THE CYCLES OF THE KINGS

Myles Dillon (1900–72), the son of John Dillon, the
nationalist politician, was educated at Belvedere
College, Dublin, Mount St Benedict, and University
College, Dublin. After receiving his doctorate from
Bonn University in 1925, he began an illustrious career
in teaching and research in Paris, Dublin, Wisconsin,
Chicago, Edinburgh, and Oxford. A pioneer in the fields
of Comparative Philology and Celtic Studies, Dillon
brought an enormous breadth of learning to every field
he studied. His publications (many of which are
addressed as much to the general reader as to the scholar)
include *The Cycles of the Kings*, *Early Irish Literature*,
The Celtic Realms (with Nora Chadwick), *Celts and
Aryans*, as well as editions of a number of Early Irish
texts. He became President of the Royal Irish Academy
in 1966, was director of the School of Celtic Studies at
the Dublin Institute of Advanced Studies, and editor of
the journal *Celtica* from 1956–72.

CELTIC STUDIES

General Editor: Professor Alfred P. Smyth, University of Kent

Aubrey Gwynn, *The Irish Church in the 11th and 12th Centuries*
edited by Gerard O'Brien

Louis Gougaud, *Christianity in Celtic Lands*

John Ryan, *Irish Monasticism*

James F. Kenney, *The Sources for the Early History
of Ireland: Ecclesiastical*

Edmund Hogan, *Onomasticon Goedelicum*

Kenneth Jackson, *Language and History in Early Britain*

D.R. Howlett, *Liber Epistolarum Sancti Patricii Episcopi:
The Book of Letters of Saint Patrick the Bishop*

Irish Antiquity
edited by Donnchadh Ó Corráin

Marie-Louise Sjoestedt, *Gods and Heroes of the Celts*

Myles Dillon, *The Cycles of the Kings*

Myles Dillon, *Early Irish Literature*

FORTHCOMING

D.R. Howlett, *The Celtic Latin Tradition of Biblical Style*

THE CYCLES
OF THE KINGS

MYLES DILLON

FOUR COURTS PRESS

This book is published by
FOUR COURTS PRESS LTD
Kill Lane, Blackrock, County Dublin, Ireland

and in North America by
FOUR COURTS PRESS LTD
c/o International Specialized Book Services
5804 NE Hassalo Street, Portland, OR 97213

First published by Oxford University Press 1946
Reprinted 1994

A catalogue record for this book is
available from the British Library.

ISBN 1-85182-178-3 pbk

Printed in Ireland by
ßetaprint Ltd, Dublin

PREFACE

OF the four cycles of Irish sagas, only the Ulster Cycle is really well known, and that as a result of Thurneysen's great study, *Die irische Helden- und Königsage*. The Fenian and Mythological Cycles have engaged the interest of modern writers and are therefore also more or less familiar. But the Historical Cycle—more properly the Cycles of the Kings, for there are a number of separate cycles—is still comparatively unknown except to a few specialists. There is no good account of it beyond what O'Curry was able to supply in his *Lectures on the Manuscript Materials of Ancient Irish History* (Dublin, 1878). The historical sagas rise sometimes to a level of emotion and expression rarely excelled in stories of the other cycles, and they contain much that is of interest for the study of political and social history.

The scope and purpose of this book are limited. It is not exhaustive. I have not attempted to do here for the Cycles of the Kings what Thurneysen did for the Ulster Cycle. Before that is possible a great deal of preliminary study must be made. Unpublished recensions of some of the texts must be published or examined, and the relation between the various recensions of a text and between different texts must be established, and a chronological order set up. There are indeed some important texts that have never been published at all. But much that has been published finds no mention here. I have chosen the stories that seem to me to have the greatest value as literature, with some regard also to their historical importance; for the book is intended not primarily for Irish scholars, but rather for the larger public whose interest may extend to this sort of knowledge, and who are not familiar with the Celtic journals. I have sought to include any details that might be of importance for students of history, anthropology or mythology, and the notes call attention to points of special interest. My chief aim has been to present the stories as well as the summary form permits, while adhering strictly to the original. Where the literary quality of a passage seemed to justify it, a literal translation is given. Almost all of the texts summarized have been translated already by others, and these translations have been of great assistance in the preparation of the summaries. But except in a few instances, as indicated in the notes, I have preferred to make fresh translations of the passages chosen. References to the standard editions and translations are supplied. Questions of manuscript tradition, sources, and date are merely presented. Here the specialist will find at least the mention of matters that await investigation. I have occasionally added a brief account of kindred sources, but without any attempt at completeness.

Proper names have been treated as seemed most convenient. 'The Battle of Moira' is familiar as the title of that story, and I have admitted the form 'Moira' into the summary. 'Brendan' is well established as a rendering of the Irish *Brénainn*. On the other hand, the names 'Cormac Mac Airt' and 'Lugaid Mac Con' have not been translated, since the Irish forms are commonly used. Different spellings of the same name, 'Derlus' or 'Durlas', 'Brandub' or 'Brandubh', reflect the varying usage of the scribes, but I have retained one form throughout each story.

Bibliographical references, when abbreviated, are given in the forms adopted by the Royal Irish Academy for the Academy's *Dictionary of the Irish Language*. Those who wish for further information about the Cycles of the Kings, or any other branch of Irish literature, should consult the excellent bibliographies compiled by R. I. Best: *Bibliography of Irish Philology and of Printed Irish Literature* (Dublin, 1913); *Bibliography of Irish Philology and Manuscript Literature: Publications 1913–1941* (Dublin, 1942). Without them I could not have written this book.

For advice and help I am indebted to my friends Eleanor Knott, Daniel A. Binchy, George Thomson and Gerard Murphy, and especially to Oliver Edwards who read the proof-sheets and suggested many improvements.

M. D.

CONTENTS

ABBREVIATIONS

AL	*The Ancient Laws of Ireland*
AU	*The Annals of Ulster*
BB	*The Book of Ballymote* (facsimile edition)
FM	*The Annals of the Four Masters*
IHS	*Irish Historical Studies*
ITS	*Irish Texts Society*
LB	*The Lebor Brecc* (facsimile edition)
LL	*The Book of Leinster* (facsimile edition)
MLR	*Modern Language Review*
PMLA	*Proceedings of the Modern Language Association*
PRIA	*Proceedings of the Royal Irish Academy*
RC	*Revue Celtique*
SG	S. H. O'Grady, *Silva Gadelica*
VSH	*Vitae Sanctorum Hiberniae* (ed. Plummer)
WB	*The White Book of Rhydderch* (ed. Evans)
YBL	*The Yellow Book of Lecan* (facsimile edition)
ZCP	*Zeitschrift für Celtische Philologie*
ZRP	*Zeitschrift für Romanische Philologie*

THE CYCLES OF THE KINGS

THE Irish took great delight in the knowledge of the past, and it was the special duty of the great order of *filid* to preserve that knowledge and to be ready to recite from it before the assemblies and at the royal banquets. They even constructed a history for Ireland from the Deluge down to the period of recorded history, and this fictitious learning is preserved in long historical poems, largely unpublished, which were later expanded in the Book of Invasions.[1] It figures also in the genealogical tables and lists of kings of which many are extant, many still unpublished. The genealogies are, however, reliable from an early time, for they quote authorities known to be as early as the sixth century,[2] and their oral tradition may go back to an even earlier period. But when it failed, the *filid* invented.

There are also a number of early historical texts: the Revolt of the *Aithechthuatha*[3] and the account of their settlements,[4] the account of the Expulsion of the Déssi,[5] the account of the death of Conn of the Hundred Battles in the Book of Lecan,[6] and that of Conall Corc and the Corcu Luígde (*v. inf.*, p. 35) and the brief tribal histories which are found in many manuscripts in association with genealogies.[7] One very early document, perhaps of the seventh century, is the Testament of Cathaer Már, a record in verse of bequests made to his sons by a king supposed to have reigned in the second century.[8] But

---

[1] D'Arbois unfortunately made this work the basis of his account of the Mythological Cycle, although it does not for the most part present ancient mythology. It is being edited by R. A. S. Macalister, *Lebor Gabála Érenn* [Irish Texts Society xxxi–xxxv], Dublin, 1938–42.

[2] Lugair Lánfili and Laidchenn are quoted in genealogies in the Book of Lecan and Rawl. B 502, s. *O'Clery Miscellany* 201, n. 2; 203; Lucreth Moccu Chiara is quoted in the Laud genealogies, ZCP 8, 307.

[3] Ed. Thurneysen, ZCP 11, 60–73; Ó Raithbheartaigh, *Genealogical Tracts* i 108–14; 122–30.   [4] Ed. Ó Raithbheartaigh, *ib.* 114–22.

[5] Ed. Meyer, *Y Cymmrodor* 14, 101; the text printed Anec. i 15–24 has taken on the form of a tale.   [6] Ed. Bergin, ZCP 8, 274.

[7] e.g. the Laud Genealogies and Tribal Histories ed. by Meyer, ZCP 8, 274.

[8] s. *O'Clery Miscellany* 201–9. An historical tract dealing with the earliest invasions of Ireland, fragments of which are preserved in the Book of Invasions, was contained in the lost manuscript of Druim Snechta, s. Thurneysen, *Zu ir. Hdschr.* 23; also MacNeill, PRIA xxvii C 123–48 (1910), whose conclusions are not confirmed by Thurneysen.

these texts, except perhaps the last named, were not apparently intended for recitation, and the mere recording of ancient history was only one part of the duties of the *filid*. It found indeed a counterpart in the work of the monks who kept in their annals a record from year to year. The great collections of annals, the oldest of which provide a contemporary account from the seventh century, are the framework of Irish history, but, strange to say, it was not until the seventeenth century that anything like a history of Ireland was written, when Geoffrey Keating compiled his splendid narrative from the fictions of the *filid*, from the mythological and historical tales, and from the annals themselves.

Apart from the documents mentioned above, the *filid* recorded history in their own way, and it was not the Greek way. Their duty was to celebrate the heroic past rather than to narrate events of recent history, and they did it in stories, with the emphasis rather on the story than on the event, so that we have a blend of fact and fiction. Sometimes the annals serve to confirm a fact. Sometimes an historical person is made the hero of a tale that is pure mythology or legend.

These 'historical' tales may be grouped into cycles around the names of the kings who appear in them, and the boundary between legend and history cannot be fixed. The earliest figure is Labraid Loingsech, supposed to have been king of Leinster in the third century B.C., hero of The Destruction of Dinn Ríg. The latest is Brian Bórama, High King of Ireland 1002–1014. And the mixture of fiction and fact varies with the period involved. This mass of historical tales is not negligible as a source for Irish history, and there are some seventy extant. But it is as literature that a selection from among them is presented here.

As literature the oldest of these stories sometimes fail by reason of the extreme bareness of the narrative. It is hardly credible for some that they were recited in the form in which they are written, for the entertainment would have lasted only a few minutes. Moreover the texts show no sign of oral tradition except where passages of obscure 'rhetoric' are recorded. We must suppose that these earliest texts are summaries of the matter of the story, and that the later transcripts first present the traditional form of the recitation. It is then the incident, the motif, the folklore, that make up their literary value, rather than any quality of form. The form was given by the *fili* in actual performance and was his personal achievement.[1]

It must be said that the distinction between these early 'historical' tales and the Ulster and Fenian cycles is arbitrary, and arrived at merely by arranging the latter in two great cycles apart. There is no tradition in favour of this arrangement. On the contrary the traditional classification was by types.[2] But the plan of modern scholars has an obvious practical value. The Ulster Cycle would fall then 'historically' between The Destruction of Dinn Ríg and the cycle of Conn of the Hundred Battles and Eogan Mór, the Fenian Cycle within the cycle of Cormac Mac Airt summarized below. No tale belonging to either of them will be included here. Moreover, some stories involving persons of the historical tales belong to the class of Adventures (*echtrai*) which is recognized both by the native tradition and by modern scholars, and these too have been excluded, except for the story of The Phantom's Frenzy (p. 11).

[1] Thurneysen, discussing the form of the early sagas, considered this possibility and rejected it, pointing out that even the early recension of *Táin Bó Cúalnge* shows a similar staccato style, s. *Heldensage* 60. But the fact that the longer syntactical periods of Middle Irish prose are lacking from the early *Táin* and other Old Irish texts does not prove that texts obviously too short for recitation as sagas were told in the form in which we have them. The very archaic text on the death of Fothath Cananne (ed. Vernam Hull, ZCP 20, 401) makes only twenty-two lines. And even some of the longer texts betray the fact that they do not record the oral tradition. Some phrases in the text of the first story presented here are in Latin.

[2] *v. inf.*, p. 115.

THE CYCLE OF LABRAID LOINGSECH

LABRAID LOINGSECH, also called Labraid Moen, was a great-grandson, according to tradition, of Úgaine Már, king of Ireland; and he, in turn, became king of Ireland *anno mundi* 4659= 341 B.C. according to the reckoning of the Four Masters.[1] The chief tale of the cycle is the story of Labraid's vengeance upon the murderer of his father. He trapped his enemy, Cobthach, with his followers, in a house of iron which was then made red hot so that all perished within.

ORGUIN DENNA RÍG
THE DESTRUCTION OF DINN RÍG

The text is Old Irish, perhaps of the ninth century, and is contained in three important MSS., LL (fcs. 269a1), Rawl. B 502 (fcs. 130b14), YBL (fcs. 112a1). The motif of the burning house recurs in the story of the *Bórama* (p. 107) and also in *Mesce Ulad*, one of the Ulster sagas (ed. Watson, p. 39). It appears in the Welsh story, *Branwen ferch Llyr* (WB 23-4 = Loth, *Mabinogion*[2] i 131).

Ed., with translation (LL, with variants from R and Y), Stokes, ZCP 3, 1-14. Numbers in brackets refer to paragraphs of Stokes's edition.

(1-4) Cobthach the Meagre, son of Úgaine the Great, was king of Bregia (north Leinster), and his brother Loegaire Lorc was king of Ireland. Cobthach was so envious of his brother that he wasted away, wherefore he was called The Meagre One of Bregia. Loegaire was summoned to visit his brother before he died, and as he came in he broke the leg of a chicken that ran on the floor. 'The sickness was unlucky for you, brother,' said Loegaire. Cobthach answered that nothing prospered with him, and asked that the chicken be brought to him that he might bind its leg.[2] He bade Loegaire return

---

[1] The Annals of Tigernach place the episode between the reign of Perdiccas of Macedonia and the death of Ezechias, king of Judaea, that is, towards the close of the eighth century B.C. (RC 16, 378), but record another tradition which would place Labraid at the close of the third century B.C. (*ib.* 394). Cathaer Már, whose reign falls in the second century A.D., is mentioned as thirtieth in succession to Labraid, *ib.* 402.

[2] A similar anecdote is told of Congal, king of Ireland and Faelán, king of Leinster in the Fragmentary Annals, edited by O'Grady, SG ii 446 (A.D. 707).

the next day to perform the funeral rites, and Loegaire consented.

' "Well," said Cobthach to his queen and his steward, "say that I died without anyone present but you, and have me placed in my chariot[1] with a razor in my hand. My brother will come eagerly to mourn me and will lie down upon me. Perhaps something will happen to him." So it was done. He is put into his chariot. His brother comes to mourn him. He goes and lies down upon him. He thrusts the knife into his back so that the point came out at the corner of his heart, and he died of it.'[2]

(5–9) Loegaire had a son Ailill Āne who held the kingdom of Leinster, and Cobthach caused him to be poisoned and took his kingdom. Ailill had a son, Moen Ollam; and he was dumb.[3] One day on the playing-field a hurley-stick struck him on the shin, and he cried out: 'I am hurt!' 'Moen is talking! (*labraid*)' said the boys, and so he was called Labraid. The men of Ireland were summoned to Tara for the assembly, and Cobthach asked them who was the most generous prince in Ireland. Craiphtine the harper and Ferchertne the poet answered that Labraid was the most generous. 'Go to him, then,' says Cobthach, 'since he is more generous than I.' 'He will be none the worse, nor you the better,' said Craiphtine. 'Begone from Ireland!' said Cobthach.

(10–13) The poet and the musician went with Labraid westwards to Scoriath, king of Fir Morca, who made them welcome. He had a daughter Moriath who was carefully guarded, for none had yet been found worthy of her. Her mother's two eyes never slept at once, but one of them always watched the girl. Moriath loved Labraid, and they had an understanding. Scoriath prepared a feast for the Fir Morca, and Craiphtine played sleep-music on his harp until the mother slept, so that the lovers met.

(14–18) Soon the mother awoke. 'Get up, Scoriath!' said

[1] This was put forward as evidence of an ancient tradition of chariot-burial by Margaret Dobbs, ZCP 8, 278–84, but Loth pointed out that there is no direct question of burial, RC 37, 366.

[2] This passage illustrates the bare style referred to above which can hardly represent the oral narrative.

[3] A variant tradition (*inf.*, p. 8) gives a reason for this defect.

she. 'Yours is an unlucky sleep! Your daughter breaths like
a wife! Listen to her sigh after her lover has left her!' Scoriath
threatened to kill the druids and poets unless his daughter's
lover was discovered. Labraid bade Ferchertne tell the truth,
so that he alone might be answerable. Ferchertne told what had
happened, and Scoriath accepted Labraid joyfully and ordered
a feast. Moriath was bestowed upon Labraid, and Scoriath said
that he would help him to recover the kingdom of Leinster.

(19–21) Scoriath called a hosting of the men of Munster,
and they attacked Dinn Ríg, the citadel of Leinster; but they
failed to take it and resorted to a ruse. Craiphtine was sent to
play sleep-music on the rampart, while the besiegers lay on the
ground with their fingers in their ears. When all within were
asleep, the men of Munster stormed the place and slew the
defenders. (Moriath was on that hosting and would not stop
her ears against her favourite music, so that she slept for a
whole day, for none dared to disturb her.)

(22–6) Then Labraid took the kingdom of Leinster and was
at peace with Cobthach. He invited Cobthach to visit him,
and a house was built for his entertainment. Strong was that
house, for it was made of iron, walls and floor and doors. The
Leinstermen were a full year building it, and father spoke not
of it to son nor mother to daughter, as the proverb says: 'Every
Leinsterman has his own secret.' Cobthach came with thirty
kings in his train, but he refused to enter the house till Labraid's
mother and his jester should go before him. Labraid went into
the house and said that fire and food and drink had been provided. Nine men seized the chain that had been attached to
the door, and dragged it out and fastened it to a pillar. Thrice
fifty forge-bellows, with four men to each bellows, were blown
till it grew hot for them in the house.

(27–9) ' "Your mother is within, Labraid!" said the warriors. "Nay, son," said she, "save your honour through me,
for I shall die at all events." Cobthach Coel is slain there
with seven hundred men and with thirty kings. *Inde dicitur*:

"Three hundred years, a great reckoning, before Christ's
birth, holy conception,—it was not brotherly, it was
wicked, Lorc was killed by Cobthach Coel.

"Cobthach Coel with thirty kings was killed by proud

Labraid of the great following, grandson of Loegaire from the sea; in Dind Ríg the host was killed."[1]

He was Moen Ollam at first, Labraid Moen afterwards. And Labraid Loingsech after he went into exile (*longais*), when he established a kingdom as far as the Ictian Sea,[2] when he brought back the many foreigners, two thousand two hundred foreigners with broad spears (*laignib*) in their hands, *et de quibus Laigin* (Leinstermen) *dicuntur.*'

The rest of the cycle of Labraid is preserved only in fragments. Three entries in *Cóir Anmann* (174, 175, 212) refer to him, and there are brief accounts in unpublished genealogies in LL (311a = 377a). He is mentioned in a seventh-century poem attributed to Find Fili[3] and in two poems by Orthanach Ua Coelláma, bishop of Kildare († 839).[4]

The notes to the famous Eulogy of Colum Cille contain traditions about Labraid that are worth attention. There were at least two other sagas, now lost, one recording the exile of Labraid referred to above, and one which told about his ears. The former, as summarized in the note, presents a different version of the Destruction of Dinn Ríg. The note is given here as translated by Stokes. The text is Middle Irish and is preserved in YBL (fcs. 75b33). It has been edited by Stokes in separate fragments, the first RC 20, 429, the second RC 2, 198.

'This Craiftine himself was the harper that Moriath had, the daughter of Scoriath, king of the Fir Morca, who are in the south of Ireland, in Munster. And 'tis this Moriath that gave love in absence to Maen ("dumb"), who is now called Labraid Loingsech ("exile"). This Labraid was a fosterling of Cobthach the Slender of Bregia, who had killed Labraid's father and grandfather in one night, and afterwards mangled them, and a piece of the heart of each was given to Maen, and a goblet of the blood of each, and he drank it.[5] Then a

---

[1] These stanzas are from a poem attributed to Orthanach Ua Coelláma († 839) which is still unpublished. It is preserved in Rawl. B 502, fcs. 50b2.

[2] *Mare Vectis*, the English Channel. Loth rejects this etymology, and prefers the suggestion of Rhys that *Ilius* (*portus*), i.e. Boulogne-sur-mer, was miswritten *Ictius* (= *Icht*), s. *Comptes rendus de l'Acad.* 1926, 71, note 1. The reference to Labraid's exile is clumsily added here so as to include a tradition recorded elsewhere which does not belong to the story.

[3] Ed. Meyer, *Alt. ir. Dicht.* i 44 (§§ 24–32). I owe the reference to Professor Chadwick.

[4] One is still unpublished (s. note 1); the other was edited by Meyer, ZCP 11, 708.

[5] This motif occurs in the Welsh story *Kulhwch ac Olwen* (WB 218b17 = Loth, *Mabinogion*[2] i 332).

mouse was caught in the house, and he was made to eat it as far as the tail.[1] "'Tis eating a mouse with its tail," says he, putting its tail up, whence the proverb, *eating a mouse with its tail*. So that was the cause of his being speechless for a long time afterwards. Then his fosterer banished him from Ireland, and his retinue was nine. He went eastward till he reached the island of the Britons and the speckled youths of the land of Armenia. Then his people bound him as a soldier to the king of Armenia, for he himself could not speak, and they said that the youth was son of the king of Ireland. And he got great honour from the king (of Armenia), and never had come to that king one who was more valiant than he. The king afterwards gave him the headship of his household: his fame reached the four quarters of the world; and he won for the king thirty lands which had not been his before. His renown was heard in Erin, and his darling, Moriath, daughter of Scoriath, heard it, and the damsel told her harper to go to Maen, "for", says she, "I have given him great love, and I cannot live unless I wed with him." "What profit is it for me to go?" says the harper, "for he never has spoken to any-one." [Said Moriath:] "Play you the harp in his presence, and haply he will speak."

'So then the harper fared forth to the place where Maen abode, and he played his harp before him, and told the harp news of the damsel. And the youth rejoiced at the harping and at the news that he heard. So then he said: "Good is the music you make, O Craif-tine"; and the king was pleased that he had (his) speech. Then he asked the king for an army to go to Ireland, and the king gave him an army, to wit, the crews of three hundred ships. And they landed at the mouth of the Boyne.

'And they were told that Cobthach the Slender was at Dinn Ríg, and no warning had preceded them, though he was near them. So then they marched to Dinn Ríg, and got under the house in which Cobthach dwelt, and killed Cobthach there *cum suis*.

'And some man in the house said: "Who is this that has attacked us and killed our people?" "The exile, the son of the king of Erin," a man outside made answer. "What, does the exile speak?" asked the same man there. "He speaks" (*labraid*), says the other. Hence he is called "Labraid Loingsech" ("the exile speaks"), for Maen ("dumb") had been his name at first.

'Then the exile seized the sovranty of Ireland, and he was the first to make broad blue lances (*laigne*), whence the Laigin ("Leinster-men") are named. And this is manifest, *ut poeta*:

'Labraid Loingsech, sufficient his number, slew Cobthach at

[1] A similar story is told of Lugaid Mac Con, p. 19.

Dinn Ríg: with a host of lances he fulfilled valour, thence the Laigin were named.

'After that he, taking Craiftine along with him, went to the stead where Moriath, daughter of Scoriath, dwelt; and then he wedded her, and afterwards she became his queen of Erin. So to testify this tale the poet (Ferchertne) said:

'The *céis* concealed not music from Craiftine's harp. It brought a death-sleep on the host. It sowed harmony between Maen and Moriath of Morca. More to her than any price was Labraid.

'Sweeter than any music is the harp that delights fierce Labraid the Exile. Though dumb as to secrets was the king, the *ceis* concealed not Craiftine's music.'

'Or this is the proper story:

'There was a king over Ireland, Labraid Lorc was his name, and thus was that Labraid, with two horse's ears on him. And every one who shaved the king used to be slain forthwith. Now the time of shaving him once drew nigh, and the son of a widow in the neighbourhood was enjoined to shave him then. That was told to the widow, and she came to the king and besought him that her son might not be slain.

'"He shall not be slain," quoth the king, "if he does not say what will be seen by him."

'"He will not say it," quoth the widow.

'Thereafter the widow's son shaved the king, and then he went to his house, and then a sickness seized him, and so great was the sickness that his head swelled, and he was (thus) for a long while, to wit, three half-years, and he could not rise for all that time, and no herb was found for him that would heal him.

'Now on a time a wizard happened to come to the (widow's) house and, as soon as the wizard beheld him, the sickness wherein he lay was revealed, and the wizard said that the son knew a secret story, and that if he told that story he would be well.

'"How shall that be done?" says the son's mother.

'"Let him go," says the wizard, "to the meeting of four roads, and let him turn sunwise, and the first tree that he meets on the right side, let him tell it the story and he will be well."

'Then the son went and did so, and he disburdened his heart, and every colour was on him; and this is the first tree which he happened on, to wit, a willow.

'Then came ruin on the harp of [the famous harper] Craiftine, and he went to cut the makings of a harp, and he cut from the very tree

to which the story had been told; and then the harper made ready
his harp, and played, and this is what it said:

> "*Two horse's ears on Labraid Lorc.*"

'And to certify that, the poet said:
> "The *cés* hid not music from Craiftine's harp."'[1]

---

[1] These two tales are given as commentary on the text *as crot cen chéis*,
YBL fcs. 75b19 = RC 20, 164. §. 20 = LH 170, 263. The meaning of *cés*
(*céis*) has not been established (cf. *Érin* 9, 53. n. 9), but it is, perhaps, the
sounding-board of the harp, cf. *nipsa cruit cin chéis*, Anec. ii 60.4. The second
story is told briefly by Keating (Bergin, *Stories from Keating's History of
Ireland*[3] 1) and thence found its way back into Irish folklore. A modern
version in English, admittedly derived from a history of Ireland read by a
schoolmaster, was heard by Patrick Kennedy and is admirably reported by
him, *Legendary Fictions of the Irish Celts*[2] 219. For Breton versions, s. RC
13, 485.

THE CYCLE OF CONN OF THE HUNDRED BATTLES AND EOGAN MÓR

CONN and Eogan Mór reigned over the northern and southern halves of Ireland respectively in the second century A.D. Eogan Mór was also known as Mug Nuadat from his having helped an architect named Nuada who was building the fort of Dún Aillinne for Dáire Barrach, king of Leinster, a son of the famous Cathaer Már.[1] And the two halves of Ireland were later called *Leth Cuinn*, 'Conn's Half', and *Leth Moga*, 'Mug's Half'. The division of Ireland between Conn and Eogan is recorded in an anecdote in the Book of Lecan, edited and translated by Vernam Hull, ZCP 19, 59. The Munster dynasty of the Eoganacht later claimed descent from Eogan.

The two principal tales of the cycle are 'The Wooing of Mo Méra' and 'The Battle of Mag Léana',[2] which tells of the defeat and death of Eogan, but neither of them is of literary importance. There is one that deserves notice on account of the interesting mythological motif of Sovranty as a woman, and of the historical information it contains. It is well known that in Irish tradition the inauguration of a king was held to be a marriage with Sovranty or perhaps with the goddess Ériu.[3] Here the form of the tale is an *echtrae* or Adventure, a class distinct from the historical sagas. But the text is of great importance for the historical tradition.

BAILE IN SCÁIL

THE PHANTOM'S FRENZY

The form of the *echtrae* was used by some scholar of the eleventh century, perhaps Dub Dá Leithe (abbot of Armagh 1049–64), to introduce a list of the kings of Ireland from Conn of the Hundred Battles to the end of the High Kingship. The compilation is preserved in Rawl. B 512 and in Harl. 5280 (only the first half). The

[1] s. Laud Genealogies, ZCP 8, 303; K. Jackson, *Cath. Maige Léana* xxviii.
[2] Both ed. by Curry for the Celtic Society (1855); the latter by Jackson, Med. and Mod. Ir. Ser. ix (1938). Jackson in his edition has reported all available MSS. of The Battle of Mag Léana, and shows that the text is not earlier than the thirteenth century.   [3] s. O'Rahilly, *Ériu* 14, 14.

list is there presented in the form of a prophecy uttered by the god Lug Mac Ethnenn in the presence of Conn. But there is an earlier text entitled *Baile Chuind Chétchathaig* in which the prophecy is apparently uttered by Conn himself.[1] The two prophecies do not agree in form or in content, for the earlier is an archaic 'rhetoric', and many of the names in the latter part of it are disguised in 'kennings'. The later text, which is here presented, appears to be a conflation of two distinct prophecies, one in the old alliterative rhetorical style, and the other in syllabic verse. Neither of these prophecies has yet been interpreted, and both are very difficult and probably corrupt. They are of considerable importance for Irish history, as more than fifty kings are mentioned, with the battles they fought, the lengths of their reigns, and the manner of their deaths.

The introduction to *Baile in Scáil*, which is the *echtrae* proper, is, however, quite straightforward, and was translated by O'Curry in his *MSS. Materials* 387 f., where the document is discussed. Thurneysen seems to think that the compilation of *Baile in Scáil* took place in the eleventh century, and that the later names were added afterwards (p. 217). The introduction may be the work of the compiler (p. 215).

Ed. without translation, Meyer, ZCP 13,371 (§§ 1–40, Rawl. B 512); Thurneysen, ZCP 20, 213 (the same); Meyer, ZCP 12, 232 (§§ 41–65, Rawl.); ZCP 3, 457 (1–41, Harl. 5280).

(1–4) One day Conn was in Tara after the other kings had departed. He went on to the rampart of Tara preceded by his three druids, Mael, Bloc, and Bluiccniu, together with Eochu, Corbb, and Cesarn the *fili*. For it was his custom to mount the rampart every day lest the people of the fairy-mounds or the Fomorians should take Ireland unawares. He saw a stone at his feet and trod upon it, and it screamed so that it was heard throughout Tara. Conn asked the *fili* why the stone had screamed and what manner of stone it was. The *fili* asked for a delay of fifty days and three. At the end of that time through his power of divination he was able to answer. *Fál* (i.e. *fo-ail* 'under-rock', i.e. 'a rock under a king') was the name of the stone. It had come from Inis Fáil to Tara in the country of Fál. It would go to Teltown where a fair of games would always be held, and any prince who should not find it on the last day

---

[1] The title suggests this, but there is no introductory statement; ed. without translation, Thurneysen, *Zu ir. Hdschr.* i 48.

of the week of the Fair of Teltown would die within the year. The number of cries that the stone had uttered under Conn's feet signified the number of kings of his seed who should be over Ireland. 'Tell them to me then,' said Conn. 'I am not destined to tell them to you,' said the druid.

(5–6) A great mist came around them so that they lost their way. They heard the sound of a horseman approaching, and then he made three casts against them. The *fili* called out a warning against violation of the king's person. The horseman ceased from casting, and welcomed Conn and bade him go with him to his dwelling. They came to a plain where there was a golden tree. There was a house thirty feet long with a ridgepole of white gold. They went into the house and saw a girl seated in a chair of crystal, wearing a gold crown. In front of her was a silver vat with corners of gold. A vessel of gold stood beside her, and before her was a golden cup. They saw the Phantom himself on his throne, and never was there seen in Tara one as wonderful as he.

(7) 'He spoke to them and said: "I am not a phantom and I am not a spectre, and I have come after death to be honoured by you, and I am of the race of Adam. My name is Lug son of Ethniu son of Smretha son of Tigernmar son of Faelu son of Etheor son of Irial son of Érimón son of Míl of Spain. And I have come to tell you the span of your sovranty and of that of every prince that will come of you in Tara for ever."'

(8–9) The girl was the Sovranty of Ireland and she gave food to Conn, the rib of an ox and the rib of a hog. The ox-rib was twenty-four feet long and eight feet from the arch to the ground. The hog's rib was twelve feet long and five feet from the arch to the ground. When she went to serve the ale, she asked to whom the cup of red ale (*dergflaith*)[1] should be given, and the Phantom answered her. When he had named every prince from the time of Conn onwards, Cesarn wrote them down in *ogam* on four staves of yew. Then the Phantom and his house disappeared, but the vat and the vessel and the staves remained with Conn. And so men speak of The Vision and

---

[1] Thurneysen points out that there is a play on the words *flaith* 'sovranty' and *laith* 'a drink', *Zu ir. Hdschr.* i 48; cf. *Cáin Adamnáin* 10, 7.

Adventure and Journey of Conn of the Hundred Battles, and The Phantom's Frenzy.

(10–65) The remainder of the text is a recitation of the dialogue between the Sovranty of Ireland and the Phantom, in which the names of more than fifty kings are given. After the name of Mael Shechlainn, who died as High King of Ireland in 1022, seven names are given: Flaithbertach (16 years), Murchadh (20 years), Oengus (22 years), Murchadh or Muiredach (13 years), Aed (16 years), Cerball or Cairell (15 years), Fergal (17 years). Then follows a period of twenty-seven years of joint kingship (*comflaithius*), and the last king of Ireland is Fland Cinuch. But none of these princes appear in history as kings of Ireland.

THE CYCLE OF LUGAID MAC CON AND
CORMAC MAC AIRT, A.D. 227

EOGAN MÓR had a son Oilill Ólom whose wife was Sadb
daughter of Conn of the Hundred Battles. Oilill had three
sons, Eogan, also called Eogan Mór, Cian and Cormac Cas.[1]
Lugaid Mac Con son of Lugaid was a foster-son of Oilill. His
father was king of Munster and was succeeded by Oilill Ólom.
According to one tradition Mac Con was a son of Sadb who
had been the wife of the elder Lugaid before she came to Oilill.
Mac Con, like Labraid Loingsech, was banished from Ireland
by his foster-father and returned to seize the kingdom for himself. At the Battle of Mag Mucrama, in which he was victorious,
Eogan Mór and Art son of Conn were slain, so that Mac Con
became king of both north and south; but each of them had
begotten a son the night before the battle, Fíacha Flat-Head
son of Eogan and Cormac son of Art.

Cormac son of Art is the most famous of the early kings of
Ireland. He is said in one text to have been the first to occupy
Tara (*inf.*, p. 26), and he reigned for forty years. He was the
wisest of men, an Irish Solomon. In the Panegyric of Cormac
he is compared to Solomon and to Octavius Augustus (SG ii 96f.).
It was during his reign that Find son of Cumall and the Fenian
warriors performed their exploits, so that the whole Fenian
cycle is in a sense a part of the cycle of Cormac. The length
of the reign of Mac Con varies in different documents. Cormac
was king of Ireland from 227 to 266 according to the Four
Masters. The date of his accession appears to fall at A.D. 219
in the Annals of Inisfallen (fcs. 8a1). According to Tigernach
he reigned for forty-two years, save two separate years during
which Tara was under the occupation of the Ulaid, RC 17,
12; 14; 16 (cf. *Teasmolad Cormaic*, SG i 89, 22, = II 96 and
inf., p. 25).

---

[1] From them are descended the three Munster dynasties, Eoganacht,
Cianacht and Dál Cais; s. Laud Genealogies, ZCP 8, 303, where Oilill is credited
with nine sons, of whom only these three had children.

CATH MAIGE MUCRAMA
THE BATTLE OF MAG MUCRAMA[1]

The story is preserved in the Book of Leinster (fcs. 288a6) and is in the style of the early sagas. A second text of the latter part (§§ 63–79) is contained in YBL (fcs. 205b12) under the title *Aided Meic Con* ('The Death of Mac Con').[2] There is, moreover, an 'historical' tract on Lugaid Mac Con in Laud 610, in which many incidents of this saga are recorded. This has been edited by Meyer, *Fianaigecht* 28; ZCP 8, 309. No study of the date of *Cath Maige Mucrama* has been made, but it can scarcely be later than the tenth century.

Ed. with translation, Stokes, RC 13, 426–74; O'Grady, SG i 310 = ii 347.

(1–5) Oilill Bare-Ear son of Mug Nuadat, king of Munster, had for wife Sadb, daughter of Conn of the Hundred Battles. She bore him three sons, Eogan, Cian, and Cormac, from whom respectively are descended the Eoganacht, the Cianacht, and Dál Caiss. Lugaid Mac Con[3] was foster-son to Oilill and Sadb, and he and Eogan were reared on the same knee and at the same breast.

'One Hallowe'en Oilill went to pasture his horses on Áne Cliach.[4] A bed was made for him on the hill. That night the hill was stript bare and none knew who stripped it. Twice it happened to him thus. He wondered at that. He sent messengers to Ferches son of Commán, a poet who dwelt on the boundary of Leinster. He was a prophet and a warrior. He came to speak with him. They both went on Hallowe'en to the hill. Oilill waits on the hill. Ferches was apart from him. Oilill falls asleep listening to the grazing of the cattle. They came out of the fairy-mound, and Eogabul son of Durgabul[5] after them, and Áne daughter of Eogabul[6] with

---

[1] A plain to the west of Athenry, County Galway. The forms *Mucríma* and *Mucrama* (with secondary shortening of the unstressed long vowel) are both supported by rhymes, s. Metr. Dinds. iii 382, 10; 384, 40. *Mucrime* is also a common spelling. The battle was fought in A.D. 195 according to the Four Masters.
[2] Ed. PMLA 60, 340.
[3] His name 'son of a dog' is explained, *Cóir Anmann* 71. He was suckled by a bitch in the house of Oilill Bare-Ear. According to one tradition Sadb was his mother, s. *Fianaigecht* p. 28.
[4] Knockany, County Limerick.   [5] Yew-fork son of Oak-fork.
[6] Áne was a daughter of Fer Fí son of Eogabul according to the Laud Genealogies, ZCP 8, 303.

a bronze lyre in her hand playing before him. Ferches went against him and dealt him a blow. Eogabul fled into the fairy-mound. Ferches strikes him with a great spear which broke his back as he came up to Oilill. Oilill lay with the girl while he was there. The woman bit his ear so that she left neither flesh nor skin on it, and none ever grew on it from that time. And Oilill Bare-Ear is his name ever since.[1]

Áne says she has been ill-used in the outrage on herself and the killing of her father, and that she will outrage Oilill in requital, for she will leave him no compensation[2] when they part.

(6–9) On another occasion Eogan and Lugaid Mac Con went to visit Art son of Conn, Lugaid's uncle,[3] while he was on a circuit of Connacht, to get horses and bridles from him. On their way they heard music in a yew tree over a waterfall. They took the musician captive, and returned to Oilill for a decision as to which of them might keep him. He was Fer Fí son of Eogabul. Oilill bade him play, and he played a sad strain so that all wept, and then a merry strain so that all laughed until their lungs were almost visible, and then a lullaby so that they slept till the same hour on the morrow. Then he disappeared, leaving the claimants disputing.

They persisted in asking for a judgement. Oilill observed that there was little profit to be had from it now, but awarded the man to Eogan; for when they found him Lugaid had said 'the music is mine!', but Eogan had said: 'mine is the musician!' Lugaid said it was a false judgement, and challenged Eogan to meet him on the battlefield at Cend Abrat a month from that day.

(10–14) A month from that day the two armies met and Mac Con went to converse with his fool before the battle. The fool, Do Dera, foresaw defeat and death for Mac Con, and offered to go himself into battle in his place, for they were much alike. If he should fall, Mac Con was to flee, but Eogan would pursue

---

[1] This passage gives an idea of the bare style of the early sagas already referred to.

[2] *athgabáil*: the word is ordinarily a legal term for 'distraint'. The meaning here is not clear to me.

[3] Lit. 'mother's brother'.

him if he caught sight of Mac Con's legs.[1] So it fell out. Do
Dera was slain, but Eogan knew it was not Mac Con and he
saw Mac Con's legs white as fresh snow through the maze of
battle. He ran after him and made a cast which struck him
in the thigh.[2] The battle became a rout, and Eogan was the
victor.

(15–31) Mac Con fled to Scotland with his tutor Lugaid
Lága son of Mug Nuadat[3], and three times nine in their company. Mac Con warned his men to obey one another as though
each were king over the other, and that none should call him
by his name, lest the king of Scotland discover his identity
and be persuaded to kill him. The king of Scotland welcomed
them, knowing not who they were, but that they were Irish-
men. A pig and an ox were provided them each day in a guest
house till the end of a year. The king marvelled at their accom-
plishments in games and in battle, and that they had no
chieftain over them. One day as he and Mac Con were playing
chess, a stranger arrived from Ireland. He was a poet. The
king asked for news of the men of Ireland, and how the reign
of Art son of Conn was prospering. The stranger said there
never was a prince in Ireland equal to him.

' "Who is king of Munster?" asks the king. "Eogan son
of Oilill, for his father is an old man." "And Lugaid Mac
Con?" said the king. "It is not known where he went when
he was banished by Eogan son of Oilill." "That is a great
pity," said the king. "Unhappy Ireland to be without him!
And Lugaid's people, how are they?" "They are not prospering," said he, "but in subjection and misery in the service
of Eogan." '

Mac Con started at this news and went out. The king observed him and knew that he was Mac Con. He planned a ruse
to prove it. The pig and the ox were brought on the hoof one
day. The king expected that when lots were cast to see who
should slaughter and dress them, Mac Con would be exempted.
But he cast his lot with the others. The king bade the steward

[1] *colptha* 'calves'. The fair skin of a prince would shine in contrast to the
swarthy unwashed skin of his soldiers.
[2] The story of this battle is told in a separate tale, The Battle of Cend Abrat,
Lec. fcs. 192a1–b35, edited PMLA 60, 10.
[3] A brother, therefore, of Oilill, and sharing in the fosterage of Mac Con.

observe who was served first, but the steward was not admitted while they were feasting. Finally he ordered mice to be killed, and that a raw mouse be laid upon the portion of each man. They were told that they would be killed unless they ate the mice. Mac Con wished ill luck to him who had ordered it, as he put the mouse into his mouth. The king observed him. All followed his example, but there was one man who vomited each time the mouse's tail came to his lips. Mac Con reproved him and he swallowed the tail.[1]

' "They obey you," said the king. "I obey them too," said Lugaid. "Are you Lugaid?" said the king. "That is my name," said Lugaid. "Welcome to you!" said the king. "Why have you hidden yourself from me?" "For fear of you," said Lugaid. "I had avenged your wrong before to-day, if I had known." "Help me even now," said Lugaid. "You shall have help indeed," said the king. "I am king of Scotland. The daughter of the king of the Saxons is my wife. I shall bring them all to avenge your wrong." "I am thankful," said Lugaid.'

(32–47) The great army invaded Ireland and many submitted to them. They came to Mag Mucrama.[2] Art son of Conn and Eogan son of Oilill agreed to give them battle. The day before the battle Eogan went to a certain blind druid, Dil Maccu Crecga of Ossory, to ask that he come and cast a spell over the enemy. Dil consented and his daughter Moncha went with him as charioteer. The druid knew from Eogan's speech that he was doomed, and bade his daughter lie with Eogan so that perchance one of his descendants might be king of Munster. By their union Fiacha Flat-Head was begotten.[3] Art spent the night before the battle with a smith of

[1] Cf. the story of Labraid, p. 8.
[2] Here there is a digression in explanation of the place-name ('plain of the counting of pigs'). Magic pigs came out of the cave of Cruachain, Ireland's gate of Hell. They left the land barren for seven years after they passed over it. They could never be counted till one day when Queen Medb caught one by the leg, and it left its skin in her hand. They were never seen again. This tradition appears in the *Dindshenchas*, s. Prose Dinds, RC 15, 470; Metr. Dinds. iii 382; but the text here does not derive from them. Moreover there is mention here of a three-headed bird, slain by Amorgein, and a flock of red birds that destroyed everything they breathed on. These were killed by the Ulaid.
[3] Here the name is explained. When his mother was in labour her father foretold that if the birth were delayed till the next day, the child's progeny

the men of Connacht, and he, likewise, foresaw defeat, for Mac Con's army was powerful and the men of Scotland and Britain had no thought of flight. Moreover, the cause of Eogan was a bad one, for Mac Con had a lawful claim against him. The smith asked Art how many children he had. Art had but one son, so the smith bade him lie with his daughter, and of this union was begotten Cormac son of Art. Art told the girl that she would bear a son who would be king of Ireland. He foretold his own death and took leave of her.

(48–58) Mac Con's plans were ready. The account of them is obscure: apparently some of his men were concealed in a pit covered with wattles.[1] But we are told that the Irish in his army were tied leg to leg with men from Scotland so that they might not flee.[2] And there were two Britons along with every Irishman. Lugaid Mac Con, Lugaid Lága, and Béinne Bruitt were at the head of one army. Art son of Conn, Eogan son of Oilill, and Corb Cacht son of Oilill were at the head of the other.

Mac Con challenged Eogan to single combat, but Eogan refused because his cause against him was bad.[3] Mac Con said that if he should fall this time, it would not be a fool taking his place, for he would rather that the dogs of Ireland should devour his body than that he stay out of Ireland any longer.

The air was black with demons waiting to drag souls to Hell. But two angels were over Art wherever he went, on account of his truths. (The battle is joined, and we are given a lively description of the conflict. Finally, the men of Scotland come out of the pit in the ground and surround the men of Ireland. Art and his men are routed. The seven sons of Oilill are slain.

would rule over Ireland for ever. She therefore sat upon a stone in the river Suir till the next morning to prevent her delivery. The child's head was flattened on the stone, and the mother died at his birth, but from him sprang the Eoganacht, cf. *Cóir Anmann* 42. But the versions are independent. A variant account in which the druid's name is Treith Mac Da Chrega was edited by Stokes from the Book of Lecan (fcs. 167b6), RC 11, 41.

A similar story was told me in Ballycroy, County Mayo, in 1933, by Pádraig Mac Meanman, about the birth of a priest, Father Manus MacSweeney, whose memory is revered in the district.

[1] The Laud text says that he hid two-thirds of his men in the ground, but there too the account is obscure (s. *Fianaigecht* 34, 14).

[2] This motif reappears in the Feast of Dún na nGéd (*inf.*, p. 64), the whole setting of which is so similar to that of this earlier story that one can hardly doubt that it has been borrowed.

[3] Cf. *sup.* and the advice given by the smith to Art son of Conn, *inf.*, p. 23.

As Béinne Britt is beheading Eogan, Lugaid Lága comes up
and is moved by affection for his brother's son.[1] He cuts off
the head of Béinne Britt so that it falls on Eogan's breast. Mac
Con sees that and reproaches him, and Lugaid Lágae promises
him the head of the king of Ireland. He goes in pursuit of Art
and slays him.)

(59–66) Then Lugaid Mac Con took the kingdom of Ireland
and reigned in Tara for seven years. He took Cormac son of
Art in fosterage. Once it happened that sheep grazed the woad
of the queen. Lugaid adjudged the sheep as forfeit for the
trespass. Cormac was a little boy and lay on a couch beside
him. He opposed the verdict, saying that it would be more
just to award the shearing of the sheep in compensation for
the shearing of the woad. The woad would grow again, and the
wool would grow again on the sheep. 'That is the true judgement,' said all, 'and it is the son of the true prince who has
given it!' At that, one side of the house, the side in which the
false judgement was given, fell down the slope. It will remain
thus for ever, The Crooked Mound of Tara.[2] For a year afterwards Lugaid was king in Tara, and no grass came out of the
ground, nor leaves on the trees nor grain in the corn. Then the
men of Ireland expelled him from the kingship, for he was a
false prince.

(67–77) Lugaid Mac Con returned to his own country with
a great following, but Lugaid Lága did not consent to return
to the place where he had opposed his own brother, but entered
the service of the son of the king whom he had slain. Mac Con
went to Oilill to tend him as befitted a foster-son. When he
reached the place, Sadb[3] put her arms around his neck and
bade him not to go in. 'Evil is the man to whom you go! He
is not forgiving.' But Oilill welcomed him saying that they
would be as father and son, since he had no son to tend him.
He put his cheek to Mac Con's cheek and pierced it with a
poisonous tooth. As Mac Con went out he met Sadb.

'"Woe is this!" said she, as she saw him.

---

[1] s. p. 18, note 3.

[2] Called *Claenferta na Claenchaingne* 'The Crooked Mound of the Unjust
Decision', Metr. Dinds. i, 16, 42; cf. Rennes Dinds., RC 15, 283, § 35. A
different explanation of the name appears on p. 106 below.

[3] Her brother Art and her seven sons had been killed in the battle.

"It is a thrust by which a king falls. A poisoned tooth has wounded you. Your appearance has changed. Sad is the last farewell."'

Then Ferches came to Oilill, and he bade him go in pursuit of Mac Con. Mac Con came to his own country. His cheek had rotted away. He leaned against a stone in presence of his men. They saw Ferches approaching and sought to shield their king, but the spear struck him in the forehead and rang against the stone behind him. Mac Con withered lifeless to the ground.

'Oilill said:

"It is thirty years since I became a worn old man: the cast of Commán's son has aroused me from my weariness."

Oilill was king of Munster for seven years after that. Some say that Lugaid Mac Con was king of Ireland for thirty years.'[1]

There is a long poem in 'The Book of the Dun Cow' in which the events of the battle of Mag Mucrama are recited. It is entitled 'The Prophecy of Art son of Conn, and his profession of Faith' (*Fástini Airt meic Cuind 7 a chretem*). An introduction in prose tells that Art was hunting one day in Mag Breg, and was in his hunting-seat at Duma Derglúachra, looking upon the view on every side, when he saw angels ascending and descending in the sky. He was filled with the grace of the Holy Ghost and the gift of prophecy came to him. He foresaw all that was about to befall him and his parting from Mac Con as a result of the battle. (Some say that it was on the following day that he went to the house of Olc Acha the smith and lay with Étain so that Cormac was begotten.) He chose to be buried in that place on account of the Faith that would be planted there. The poem includes a prophecy of the coming of St. Patrick. This text was edited by MacNeill, PRIA iii C 532 (1895). It is also printed, LU 9822–90.

Another poem on the battle is preserved in LL (fcs. 27a36). It belongs to the class known as Dindshenchas, and is an explanation of the name of a magic yew called 'The Yew of the Disputing Sons'. Here the cause of the feud between Eogan and Mac Con is a tree which Fer Fí caused to appear to them, and Cian, Eogan's brother,

---

[1] So *Aided Meic Con* ('The Death of Mac Con'), PMLA 60, 342 (YBL fcs. 205b12); the Annals of Tigernach give alternative traditions: *Ailii aiunt Lugaid Mac Con post hoc bellum in Temporia regnase [annis xviii] uel XXX ut alii aiunt*, RC 17, 11. In the LL text of The Battle of Crinna the period is twenty-seven years, LL fcs. 328f16 (SG ii 491). In *Baile In Scáil* it is twenty-five years, ZCP 20, 222, 10.

is also involved. Oilill awards the tree to Eogan, and Mac Con
challenges Oilill to battle at Cend Febrat, and is there wounded so
that he was lame afterwards. Then the battle of Mag Mucrama and
the death of Art are mentioned.[1]

A text preserved in Edinburgh XXVIII (p. 11, 14th century?)
tells the lamentations of Oilill Ólom for each of his seven sons,
and the reproach he uttered against Sadb for her joy in the victory
of her son Mac Con. The narrative is modern Irish, but the rhetorical passages are old. It is still unpublished.[2]

GEINEAMAIN CORMAIC
The Birth of Cormac

The birth of the famous Cormac son of Art is told in the story of
the Battle of Mag Mucrama. The story of his birth is told as a single
episode in YBL (fcs. 180a48–181b25, 14th century) and in the Book
of Ballymote (fcs. 260a16–b44, 14th century). It is later in its extant
form than *Cath Maige Mucrama*, perhaps not much earlier than the
manuscripts, but it represents the source upon which the author has
there drawn, for there is close verbal agreement in the parallel
passages. BB presents a text almost identical with that of YBL
and may have been copied from it. The succeeding folios in both
manuscripts also carry identical texts.

Ed. with transl. (BB), O'Grady, SG i 253 = ii 286. The text of
Y is still unedited.

Art son of Conn of the Hundred Battles went westwards
across the Shannon with a great army to fight the battle of
Mag Mucrama. He spent the night before the battle in the
house of Olc Acha the smith. Olc Acha reproached him,
saying that it was not right for him to do battle against Mac
Con, nor for Eogan; for Eogan's cause was bad in that Lugaid
had a lawful claim against him. In answer to his question
Art said he had but one son, and Olc Acha bade him lie
with his daughter Étain. Art lay with her and told her she
would bear a son who would be king of Ireland. He foretold his
death and departed bidding her bring the boy for fosterage
to his friend Lugna Fer Trí in Corann.

Étain was then pregnant and resolved to go to the house of
Lugna Fer Trí so that her child should be born there. When
she reached his country the birth-pains seized her, and she got

---

[1] Ed. *Ériu* 14, 154.
[2] A modern recension (*Nuallghubha Oiliolla Óluim i ndiaidh a chlainne*)
was published in *The Gaelic Journal* 18, 75.

down from her chariot and was delivered of a son on a bed of ferns. A peal of thunder greeted his birth, and Lugna, hearing this, knew that it was for the birth of Cormac son of the true prince Art, and he set out in search of him.

Étain slept after her delivery, and entrusted the boy to her maid till they should continue their journey. The maid fell asleep, and a she-wolf came and carried off the child to her lair in the place now known as Cormac's Cave. When the mother awoke she cried out for grief. Lugna came to where she lay, and she told him all that had happened. He brought her to his house, and proclaimed that whosoever should find tidings of the child should obtain in reward whatever he asked.

Grec Mac Arod was abroad one day, and coming upon the cave he saw the whelps playing before it and the child creeping among them. He brought the news to Lugna, and was granted the territory where the Grecraige now dwell. The child and the whelps were brought home from the cave, and the child was named Cormac, for that was the name his father had given him. He was the delight of many for his beauty and eloquence and grace and dignity and strength and judgement.

One day, as he was playing with Lugna's sons, he struck one of them. The lad exclaimed that it was too much to suffer a blow from one whose race and kindred were unknown, save that he was a fatherless child.[1] Cormac complained to Lugna, and Lugna told him that he was the son of the true prince, Art son of Conn of the Hundred Battles, and that it was prophesied that he should steer his father's rudder, for there would be no prosperity in Tara until he should reign there. 'Let us go', said Cormac, 'to seek recognition in my father's house in Tara.' 'Let us go then,' said Lugna.

They went to Tara, and Mac Con welcomed them and took Cormac into fosterage. There was a woman hospitaller in Tara at that time named Bennaid. Her sheep grazed the queen's woad. Mac Con awarded the sheep to the queen in compensation for the woad. 'No,' said Cormac. 'The shearing of the sheep is enough in compensation for the grazing of the woad, for both will grow again.' 'It is the true judgement!' said all. 'It is the son of the true prince who has given judge-

---

[1] This motif occurs in the Wooing of Étain (*Heldensage* 599), and in the Voyage of Mael Dúin (RC 9, 456, 1).

ment!' The side of the house on which the false judgement had been given fell down the slope. It will stay thus for ever. That is The Crooked Mound of Tara.

The men of Ireland expelled Mac Con and gave the kingship to Cormac. Everything prospered while he lived. His wolves[1] remained with him, and the reason for the great honour he received was that he had been reared by wolves.[2]

Tara was restored by Cormac so that it was grander than ever before, houses, fences, and buildings. Well was it with Ireland in his time. The rivers teemed with fish, the woods with mast, the plains with honey, on account of the justice of his rule. Deer were so plentiful that there was no need to hunt them.[3] Cormac built the noblest building that ever was raised in Tara.[4] Though he was opposed by the Ulstermen he was never deprived of the kingship till his death. He died in the *ráith* of Spelán the hospitaller in Cletech[5] when a salmon bone stuck in his throat.

Cormac ordered that he should not be buried in Bruig na Bóinne, for he did not adore the same god as those who were buried there.[6] He ordered his burial in Ros na Ríg with his face due east towards the rising sun.

The tradition concerning the attack upon Cormac by the Ulstermen, and his victory with the aid of Tadg son of Cian son of Oilill Ólom, is recorded in an historical tract inserted in the Leinster genealogies (LL fcs. 328b–329a), edited by O'Grady in the Appendix to *Silva Gadelica* (ii 491–3). We have also a late form of the saga, entitled 'The Battle of Crinna' (*Cath Crinna*), in the Book of Lismore, which O'Grady edited too (SG i 319 = ii 359), but it is not of great account.

ESNADA TIGE BUCHET

THE MELODIES OF BUCHET'S HOUSE

This charming story dates from the tenth century, and is preserved in five vellum manuscripts, including LL (fcs. 270a45), Rawl. B 502 (fcs. 133b31) (both 12th century) and YBL (fcs. 113a47).

---

[1] Here the word is *coin* 'hounds'.   [2] *conaib.*

[3] For a panegyric of Cormac, s. O'Grady, SG i 89 = ii 96.

[4] For a description of Cormac's house at Tara, s. Metr. Dinds. i 30–6.

[5] A place close to New Grange, on the Boyne River, s. Hog. Onom. It was the royal seat of Muirchertach Mac Erca († 534), s. RC 23, 395.

[6] He is here credited with foreknowledge of the Christian faith.

Ed. with transl. (L with variants), Stokes, RC 25, 18.[1]

There was a hospitable man in Leinster named Buchet. He had Eithne, the daughter of Cathaer Mór, king of Ireland, in fosterage. Cathaer had twelve sons, and they used to come for guesting with large companies, so that they wasted all Buchet's substance. At last he was left with only seven cows and a bull, where there had been seven herds of cattle.

Buchet went to Cathaer to seek redress. But Cathaer was then a withered old man and told him that he could not restrain his sons, and advised him to go away. Buchet fled secretly in the night until he came to Kells of the Kings. He brought with him only his old wife, his seven cows and the bull, and the girl, Eithne daughter of Cathaer. They dwelt in a hut in the forest, and the girl served them.

Cormac was in Kells at that time, for he had not yet taken the kingship of Ireland. Medb of the Red Side, the wife of Art, took the kingship after Art's death and did not suffer Cormac.[2] Kells was then the royal seat, and it was Cormac, when he became king, who founded Tara on the land of Odrán, a herdsman.[3]

One day, when he was king, Cormac saw the girl milking the cows. She put the last milk into a vessel apart. Then she cut rushes and put the best rushes in a separate bundle. She drew water and put the water from the middle of the stream in a separate pail.

   ' "Who are you, girl?" said Cormac. "The daughter of a poor herdsman yonder," she said. "Why do you divide the water and the rushes and the milk?" "A man who was honoured formerly," said she, "to him I bring the freshest of the rushes and the last of the milk, and the rest is for myself, so that he may not be without honour so far as I can find. And if I should find greater honour he should have it." "It

---

[1] A verse recension in Rawl. B 502 (fcs. 87a1), which derives from the prose, has been edited by Mary Hayden, ZCP 8, 261.
[2] This conflicts with the tradition concerning Lugaid Mac Con in the preceding stories.
[3] This conflicts with all established tradition. Cormac's father, Art, and his grandfather, Conn of the Hundred Battles, dwelt at Tara, and Tuathal Techtmar long before them (s. pp. 57, 103). The sentence seems to be a gloss that has crept into the text, for we have just been told that Cormac was at Kells because he was not yet king.

may be that you shall find it," said Cormac. "Whom do you
honour so?" "His name is Buchet," she said. "Is that
Buchet of Leinster?" said Cormac. "It is he," she said.
"Are you Eithne of the Long Side, daughter of Cathaer
Mór?" said Cormac. "Yes," said she.'

Cormac sent a message to Buchet to ask for the hand of
Eithne, but he did not give her for he was not her father. She
was carried off that night, and spent one night with Cormac.
Next day she escaped, but that night she had conceived a
son, Cairpre Lifechar son of Cormac.

Afterwards she became Cormac's queen, but only when her
bride-price had been paid to Buchet. And Cormac gave him
all that he could see from the rampart of Kells for a whole
week, cow and man and ox and horse, so that Buchet was
unable to bring all his wealth of herds back into Leinster.

'The music of Buchet's house was his laughing cry to his
guests: "Welcome! You will be happy, and I shall be happy
along with you!" Fifty warriors made music when the guests
were drunk. Fifty maidens too played for the company.
And then fifty harpers soothed the guests until morning.
And so men speak of "The Melodies of Buchet's House".'

BAILE BINNBÉRLACH MAC BUAIN

BAILE OF THE CLEAR VOICE SON OF BUAN

There is another love-story that is worth recording here. It
belongs, however, to the time of Cormac's father, Art son of Conn
of the Hundred Battles. The text is preserved only in three late
vellums, Harl. 5280 (f. 48a, 16th century), RIA 23 N 10 (p. 129,
16th century), and TCD H. 3, 18 (p. 47, 16th century), but the
language of the first seems not later than the tenth or eleventh
century, even if we allow for deliberate archaism. That of H includes some later forms. The text of N is unpublished.

Ed. with transl., Meyer, RC 13, 220 (Harl.), and O'Curry, MSS.
Mat. 472 (H. 3, 18). Numbers refer to lines of Meyer's edition.

(1–30) Baile of the Clear Voice was the only son of Buan
grandson of Caba. He was the chosen lover of Ailinn, daughter
of Lugaid son of Fergus of the Sea, and he was beloved of all
who saw him or heard of him, both men and women. Baile
came south from Emain Macha with his companions. When

they had reached the trysting-place and were making merry, they saw a fearful spectre approaching from the south, darting like a hawk from the cliff or like the wind from a grey sea. His left side was towards them.[1] They accosted him and asked for news. He said that he had come north from Mount Leinster, and had no news save only that Ailinn had given her love to Baile and was on her way to meet him, when she was over-taken and killed by the warriors of Leinster. Druids and seers had foretold that they would not meet in life, but that they would meet after death, never to part.

Baile died of grief, and he was buried and his tomb was raised and his funeral games were held by the Ulstermen. And a yew tree grew out of his grave, and the likeness of Baile's head was in its branches.

(31–44) Then the spectre went south to where Ailinn was. She asked for news. He said he was going to Mount Leinster and had no news save only that he had seen the Ulstermen dig the grave of Baile son of Buan, heir to the kingdom of Ulster, and celebrate his funeral games; for he had died on his way to meet a girl to whom he had given his love. Ailinn fell dead, and she was buried, and out of her grave there grew an apple-tree. After seven years it was a strong tree, and the likeness of Ailinn's head was in its branches.

(45–75) After seven years poets and seers cut down the yew that was over Baile's grave, and made a poet's tablet from it, and the vision-tales and feasts and loves and wooings of Ulster were written on it. Likewise the wooings of Leinster were written on the wood of the apple-tree. When the feast of Samain was held by Art son of Conn, the poets and men of every craft came, and brought their tablets with them. The two tablets were brought to him, and as he held them face to face they sprang together and were joined like woodbine round a branch. It was impossible to part them. They were kept in the treasury at Tara with all the other treasures, until Dúnlang son of Énna burned them, when he slew the maidens.[2]

The story of Cormac's Adventure in the Land of Promise does not belong to the Historical Cycle, nor does the whole body of Fenian tradi-

---

[1] A sign of evil.

[2] This event is recorded in the *Annals of Tigernach*, RC 17, 13, and in the *Annals of the Four Masters* i 114 (A.D. 241). *Cf. inf.* p. 105.

tion which falls chronologically in the cycle of Cormac. One famous text is the *Tecosca Cormaic* (Instructions of Cormac), a collection of precepts addressed to his son Cairpre.[1] The text dates from the Old Irish period (early 9th century) and is one of a whole group of similar gnomic collections which do not fall within the scope of this book. The attribution of these sayings to Cormac, the Irish Solomon, was no doubt prompted by the Book of Proverbs in which King Solomon addresses his son.

[1] Ed. Kuno Meyer, *RIA Todd Lecture Series* xv.

THE CYCLE OF CRIMTHANN SON OF FIDACH, A.D. 366

CRIMTHANN son of Fidach became king of Ireland in 366 in succession to Eochu Muigmedón son of Muredach Tírech. He is called 'king of Ireland and Albion as far as the Ictian sea' in *Cormac's Glossary* (883). His death is recorded by the Four Masters s. a. 378. Keating gives a brief account of his reign.[1] The cycle associated with his name includes a number of tales, one of which gives an account of his death, another having for hero Conall Corc who was king of Munster during his reign.

AIDED CRIMTHAINN MAIC FIDAIG 7 TRÍ MAC N-ECHACH MUIGMEDÓIN .I. BRIAN, AILILL 7 FIACHRA
THE DEATH OF CRIMTHANN SON OF FIDACH AND OF THE THREE SONS OF EOCHU MUIGMEDÓN, BRIAN, AILILL AND FIACHRA

The story has no literary merit. It is included here as being of interest for political and social history. Indeed it may be no more than a running commentary on the passages of historical poetry quoted which are earlier in language than the prose. The text is preserved in YBL (fcs. 186a12) and BB (fcs. 263b21), and belongs perhaps to the eleventh century.

Ed. with translation, Stokes, from YBL with variants from BB, omitting verse passages, RC 24, 174–89; O'Grady, from BB alone, SG i 330 = ii 373. Numbers refer to paragraphs of Stokes' edition.

(1–2) Eochu Muigmedón son of Muredach Tírech was king of Ireland, and his wife was Mongfind daughter of Fidach. She bore four sons, Brian, Fiachra, Ailill and Fergus. Once in a dream she saw them changed into animals, Brian as a lion, Fiachra as a greyhound, Ailill as a beagle, Fergus as a cur. They were fighting, and at first the greyhound would sometimes overcome the lion, but in the end the lion subdued the other three, and they submitted to him. Mongfind told her dream to Sithchenn the druid, and he explained it. Brian and Fiachra would be rivals, and for a time the kingship would alternate between their descendant lines, but the line of Brian would

---

[1] P. Dinneen, *The History of Ireland by Geoffrey Keating* ii 369–71 [Irish Texts Society VIII].

finally prevail. Ailill would strive to win territory from his kinsmen. But Fergus would beget only a churl, and his race would be almost unknown.

(3–8) When Eochu died there was a struggle between his five sons for the succession, Niall[1] on the one side and the four sons of Mongfind on the other. Since Brian, her favourite, could not secure the kingship, Mongfind persuaded the men of Ireland by entreaty and by sorcery, for she was skilled in witchcraft, to give it to her brother Crimthann. And Brian went to Scotland[2] to learn the art of warfare from Senoll son of Ongae. After seven years he returned, strong and skilled in warfare, and Crimthann was still king. Crimthann then went to Scotland on his royal circuit; for thus used the king of Tara to proceed on royal circuit: from Tara into the province of the Gailióin (i.e. Leinster), and from there to the two provinces of Munster, then into Cóiced Ól nÉcmacht (i.e. Connacht), then to the province of Ulster,[3] and from there to Scotland.[4] During his absence the sons of Mongfind divided his kingdom between them, and Crimthann hastened back and raised an army in Connacht to expel his sister's sons. Mongfind, however, planned a treacherous feast to which she invited him, as though to make peace between her sons and her brother. She gave him there a poisoned cup, and he refused to drink it until she had first drunk of it. Mongfind drank and Crimthann drank after her. Mongfind died on the eve of Samain, so that the common people call Samain the feast of Mongfind; for she was powerful while she lived, and women and common folk pray to her on Samain eve. Crimthann died on his way home to Munster.[5] (Here follows a poem beginning: *Fertán Crimthainn cid dia tá.*)

(9–14) The treachery of Mongfind and the sacrifice of her own life were of no avail, for it was Niall who took the kingship in succession to Crimthann, and Brian was his 'smiter in battle', seizing hostages and levying tribute from all parts of the kingdom. Brian became king of Connacht, and Fiachra took

---

[1] His mother was Cairenn Chasdub, s. p. 38.

[2] So did Cú Chulainn in *Tochmarc Emire*.

[3] This division is the same as that in 'The Feast of Dún na nGéd', s. p. 60.

[4] This is an anachronism, for the Irish kingdom in Scotland was not established till the end of the fifth century; but it is significant for the tradition of a later period.   [5] FM 378.

a territory extending from Carn Feradaig to Mag Mucrama; but enmity arose between them. Brian defeated Fiachra in battle and sent him captive to Niall, but was himself later slain by Crimthann son of Énna Cennselach: Fiachra was then released and became king of Connacht and 'smiter in battle' to Niall.

(15–17) Ailill and Fiachra went to levy tribute and take hostages from Munster. They were opposed by Eochaid son of Crimthann and by Maide Meschorach at the head of the Men of Munster and the Érainn. A battle was fought at Caenraige[1] in which Ailill and Fiachra were victorious, but Fiachra was badly wounded and died on his way back. The hostages taken were buried alive around his grave as a reproach to the men of Munster for ever and a triumph over them. (Here follows a poem beginning: *Maicne Echach ard a nglé*.)

(18–19) When the Men of Munster heard of Fiachra's death, they set out, and Ailill was seized by Eochaid son of Crimthann, king of Munster,[2] for it was natural for them to take captive the son of the woman who had killed their lord (Crimthann, son of Fidach), a man who had brought all Ireland and Scotland under the dominion of Munster. Ailill was killed by them. There was a long war between Munster and Connacht after that, and it resulted in the struggle for the territory which is now North Munster, and was the cause of all the later warfare between the two provinces. (Here follows a poem beginning: *Tri maic Echach na ngním ngrinn*.)

The remaining passage of prose is purely historical and marks the doubtful character of this text, whether saga or mere commentary on historical poems.

(20) Lugaid Menn son of Oengus Tírech son of Fer Corp was the first to take the territory of North Munster by force. There are two territories which the Men of Munster defended by force, Ossory which was seized in compensation for Eterscél who was killed by the Men of Leinster, and North Munster in compensation for the death of Crimthann. But they are not lawfully entitled to them, for that territory of North Munster

---

[1] This battle is not recorded in the Annals so far as I can see.

[2] 'king of Ireland' in the text, but this must be an error. No king of Munster was king of Ireland after Niall of the Nine Hostages until the usurpation of Brian Bórama in 1002.

belongs to Connacht according to the law dividing the provinces, since Connacht extends from Limerick to Drowse.[1]

ERCHOITMED INGINE GULIDI

THE EXCUSE OF GULIDE'S DAUGHTER

The brief episode described here seems to be merely the occasion for a display of eloquence, *ségantus bríathar* as it is called in the text. It is of no literary merit nor has it any great value from the point of view of history. It is just another fragment of tradition. Perhaps its chief interest is linguistic. An exact translation would be a difficult task. The text is preserved in Rawl. B 512 (15th century). It is early Middle Irish, perhaps of the eleventh century.

Ed. with translation, Meyer, Hib. Min. 65–9.

(1–2) Fedlimid son of Crimthann became king of Munster. Once he went on a circuit of Munster and came into West Munster as far as Áth Lóchi, where Gulide the satirist lived. It was in the depth of winter and the snow was so deep that the king's retinue found it difficult to make their way. Fedlimid inquired who lived nearest, and the guides replied that it was his friend Gulide of Áth Lóchi. Fedlimid said that he was bitter, fierce, and given to hard words, quick to ask a favour and slow to grant one. Yet Gulide had accepted gifts of gold and silver, horses, bridles, and saddles, and they were entitled to his hospitality for the night. The company went therefore to his house, and horns and trumpets were sounded on the rampart of the enclosure. Only Gulide and his daughter were within, for he was a grey-haired old man of seven score years.

(3–8) Gulide had been a great warrior, a great hospitaller, and a great satirist, so that he was known as Gulide the Satirist. He rose from where he lay and leaned on his elbow to look around, but he saw only his daughter. He bade her go out to see who was come. She went out and came back with the news that a great company was there, and that she thought it was Fedlimid son of Crimthann with the chiefs of the Men of Munster. 'Go out to the company,' said Gulide, 'and make a fine speech (*ségantus bríathar*) so that they may pass on from us to-night.'

[1] In south County Donegal.

The girl went out and spoke to Fedlimid. Her speech contains many obscure words, but the burden of it is that when Gulide was prosperous he did not grudge Fedlimid hospitality for three days or five or ten or a month or even a year, however great his retinue. Now, however, the times are bad, too many guests pass that way and his estate is poor. There is no food in the house. The girl apologizes finally for her poor speech and wishes that her three elder sisters might have been there to speak in her stead. But Fedlimid is delighted with her eloquence, and bestows upon her the land from Drong to Loch Léin.

(9–10) The girl says that she once went on a visit and received poor entertainment, the twenty-fourth part of the mouldy skin of a scabby calf, a little oats from the north end of a field that had gone back to meadow,—neither sun nor wind had ripened it, it had been reaped before it should have been reaped and ground before it should have been ground, and so forth. Here again much is obscure. Finally she says that Fedlimid will not be treated so. He shall get hospitality for the night, even if it be a wet covering in half-roofed houses, with bread half-stale and joints half-bare.

Then the girl took Fedlimid by the hand and led him inside. He was there for three days and three nights, and never was he better fed as long as he was king. And Fedlimid left them his blessing.

LONGES CHONAILL CHUIRC

The Exile of Conall Corc

To this cycle belongs also the saga of Conall Corc, but we have only one text in saga-form, and it is incomplete in the single manuscript that contains it.[1] Conall Corc became king of Munster in succession to Crimthann son of Fidach who was his foster-father and died childless. When Conall was an infant his palm was read by a diviner (*fer spirdo*),[2] who foretold that if he released captives whenever he could, his race would be famous and would bear his name. Later when he grew up, Crimthann sent him into Leinster to levy a tribute of sixty cows. While there he ransomed three captives,

---

[1] Professor Vernam Hull informs me that the text in TCD H.3.17, col. 768, described by Gwynn (*Cat.* 358) as 'the story of the finding of Cashel', is a different story.

[2] This is the only reference to palmistry in Irish literature so far as I know.

one of them a certain Gruibne who escaped to Scotland. Then Corc, like Lugaid Mac Con in the Battle of Mag Mucrama and Máel Fothartaig in *Fingal Rónáin*, was banished to Scotland through the malice of the king's wife, because he had refused to be her lover. Crimthann had written a doom in secret *ogam* upon his shield, but when he arrived in Scotland, a servant of Gruibne deciphered the message and altered it to mean a request for honourable treatment. Gruibne brought Corc to Feradach Findfechtnach, king of the Picts, who gave him his daughter in marriage. After ten years Corc returned to Munster, and the day that he reached Ireland was the day of Crimthann's death. He then became king of Munster. All this is told in an old historical tract, probably of the early eighth century, printed without translation, Anec. iii 57–63.

The extant fragment of the saga is preserved in LL (fcs. 287a1) and seems to belong to the eighth or ninth century. It has been edited with a translation, and a discussion of other references to Conall Corc, by Vernam Hull, PMLA 56, 937–50.

1. Conall Corc came to Dublin and saw ships about to sail. He went with them eastwards till he saw the mountains of Scotland, where he went ashore. He went on to a mountain. A heavy snow fell, and he was without food for six days. He fell lifeless in the valley, and was discovered there by Gruibne who had come in search of his pigs.

' "A dead man," said he. Then he saw that his body was warm. "The man has been frozen," said he. "Kindle a fire around him so that his limbs may not break as he rises." That is done until he steamed. He got up suddenly. "Peace, warrior," said Gruibne. "Do not be afraid." '

2. Then Gruibne recognized Conall Corc and greeted him with a long 'rhetoric'. The text says: 'It chanced that he was one of the prisoners that Corc had delivered from the Leinstermen, the poet who spoke the poetry (*filidecht*).' He embraced him, and inquired who had written the *ogam* on his shield, for it was not auspicious. He told Corc that it meant: 'If you come to Feradach by day, your head shall be off before evening. If you come by night, your head shall be off before morning.' 'It shall not happen so,' says Gruibne.

3. Gruibne brought Conall to his house on a litter. A month later he went to Feradach and told him that he had found a man dead, and that his shield bore a message in *ogam* which

read: 'This is the son of the king of Munster who has come. If he should come by day, give him your daughter before evening; if by night, let her sleep with him before morning.' 'It is sad,' said Feradach. 'Alas that you did not find him alive!' Gruibne then pledged the king in the amount of Conall's weight in silver, and brought Conall in. The king gave him a great welcome, but he would not give his daughter to a soldier in exile. However they came together, and the woman became pregnant and bore him a son. She did not admit whose son it was, and she was about to be burned, for that was the penalty for a girl's sin. But the men of Scotland begged a year's respite for her until the child should show the form, voice, and manner of his kin.[1]

4. 'They come to burn her at the end of the year. "I shall not give you your son," said she. "Nay, you shall do so," said he, "in the presence of Feradach." Then when they were about to burn her, she gave him to him before them both. "Is the boy by Corc, woman?" said Feradach. "Yes," said the woman. "I will not accept him from you," said Corc, "for he is a bastard until his grandfather bestow him." "I give him to you, then," said Feradach. "The boy is yours," "I will accept him now," said Corc. "Begone, woman," said Feradach, "and bad luck to you!" "She shall not go," said Corc, "for she is not guilty." "But she is guilty," said Feradach. "She is not guilty," said Corc. "To every son belongs his mother. The guilt rests upon her son, upon her womb."[2] "Let the boy be cast out!" said Feradach. "He shall not be cast out," said Corc, "for that child is not of man's estate. The boy will pay the penalty of his guilt." "They are both saved," said Feradach. "It was lucky," said Corc. "Well, Corc," said Feradach, "sleep with your wife. You are he whom we should have chosen, if we were choosing. I shall pay her bride-price to the Men of Scotland." '

5. Conall stayed in Scotland until his wife had borne three sons. Then Feradach bade him return to his own country with

---

[1] Hull refers to AL V 454, 458 where this phrase occurs. These three tests were used in the case of doubtful paternity, to decide who was the father of the child. Presumably the girl in this case was expected then to declare the identity of the father, as indeed she did.

[2] Cf. Thurneysen, *Irisches Recht* § 28; Thurneysen and others, *Studies in Early Irish Law* 161.

his wife and sons, giving him as much silver as three men could carry, and a company of thirty warriors. As they arrived in Munster snow fell so that they lost their way. The swineherd of Aed, king of Múscraige, was tending his swine that day, and at night he told the king of a wonderful sight that he had seen. He saw a yew tree upon a rock,[1] and an oratory in front of it with a flagstone at the threshold, and angels ascending from the flagstone and descending upon it.[2] A druid interpreted the vision. That place would be the residence of the king of Munster for ever, and the first man to kindle fire under that yew-tree would be the ancestor of the kings of Munster.

6. Aed wished to go there at once, but the druid advised him to wait until morning. Meanwhile Conall came by chance to the place and kindled a fire for his wife and sons, so that Aed found him there next day beside the fire with his sons about him. He welcomed him and gave him his son as a hostage. It was just then that there was rivalry for the kingship of Munster, upon the death of Crimthann. Conall established himself at Cashel and he was king of Munster within a week.

7. The first hostage that the king of Munster took was the hostage of Múscraige, and he set him free and took a queen from there to Cashel. The swineherd was given freedom for himself and his children from tax and service. It is he who proclaims the king of Cashel and receives the king's garment. Therefore the place is called *Cassel Cuirc* ('The Castle of Corc'), and the seed of Corc son of Lugaid are in Cashel for ever from that time.

---

[1] This was, of course, the Rock of Cashel.   [2] Cf. *Gen.* xxviii 12.

THE CYCLE OF NIALL OF THE NINE HOSTAGES
A.D. 379

NIALL of the Nine Hostages, son of Eochu Muigmedón, was king of Ireland from A.D. 379 to 405. His death is recorded by the Four Masters *s. a.* 405. The epithet is explained by a tradition, cited by Keating, that Niall took five hostages from Ireland, one from each province, and four from Scotland.[1] From him are descended the northern and southern Ui Néill ('Descendants of Niall') who held the High Kingship in alternate succession for more than six hundred years.

ECHTRA MAC N-ECHACH MUIGMEDÓIN

THE ADVENTURES OF THE SONS OF EOCHU MUIGMEDÓN

One of the stories about Niall contains the motif of the evil-looking hag who is transformed by his kiss into a lovely maiden and reveals herself as the hypostasis of Sovranty. This incident recurs in an anecdote about Lugaid Láigde, father of Lugaid Mac Con, *Cóir Anmann* 70, cf. Metr. Dinds. iv 138–42 (s. *Ériu* 14, 17). Stokes draws attention to parallels in *The Marriage of Sir Gawain*, the story of Florent in Gower's *Confessio Amantis*, and Chaucer's *Wife of Bath's Tale* (*Academy* xli 399; 425). The story is preserved in YBL (fcs. 188a41) and BB (fcs. 265a1). It cannot be earlier than the eleventh century, for Brian Bórama († 1014) is mentioned. It is the subject of a poem by Cuán Ó Lothchain († 1024), edited by Maud Joynt, *Ériu* 4, 91.

Ed. with translation, Stokes, RC 24, 190 (Y with variants from B); from BB only, with translation, O'Grady, SG i 326 = ii 369.

(1–4) Eochu Muigmedón, king of Ireland, had five sons, Brian, Ailill, Fiachra, Fergus and Niall. Mongfind ('Fair Hair') daughter of Fidach was his queen and the mother of four sons, but Niall was the son of Cairenn Chasdub daughter of Scal the Dumb, king of the Saxons. Mongfind hated Niall and his mother, and inflicted much hardship upon Cairenn, who was compelled to draw water from the well.[2] Even when she was pregnant with Niall she was compelled to do it, and the

---

[1] s. P. Dinneen, *The History of Ireland by Geoffrey Keating* ii 411–13.

[2] Cairenn was evidently in the position of secondary wife which was recognized under Irish law, s. Thurneysen and others, *Studies in Early Irish Law* 84.

child was born in the open as she lay beside her pail. She dared not take up the child, but left it there, and none dared take it up for fear of Mongfind. Then Torna the Poet came by and took up the child, and he foresaw all that was to come. He took him and reared him, and neither he nor the child came to Tara until Niall was of age to be king.

'Then Torna and Niall came to Tara. Cairenn met them as she was carrying water. Niall said to her: "Leave that menial work!" "I do not dare," said she, "on account of the queen." "My mother shall not be a servant," said he, "and I the son of the king of Ireland!" He took her with him to Tara, and dressed her in a purple robe.'

(5–8) Mongfind was angry and called upon Eochu to judge between his sons as to who should succeed him. He referred the matter to Sithchenn the smith, who was a prophet.[1] Sithchenn set fire to a forge in which the five sons were at work. Niall came out carrying the anvil, Brian brought the hammers, Fiachra brought a pail of beer and the bellows, Ailill brought the weapons, and Fergus a bundle of kindling with a stick of yew in it. Sithchenn greeted Niall as the victor, and appraised the others according to their merits. Fergus was pronounced sterile, and hence the proverb 'a stick of yew in a bundle of kindling'.

(9–17) One day the five sons went hunting and they lost their way in the forest and were enclosed on every side. They lit a fire and cooked some of their game and ate till they were satisfied. They wanted water, and Fergus set out in search of it. He found a well, but there was an old woman guarding it. She was as black as coal. Her hair was like a wild horse's tail. Her foul teeth were visible from ear to ear and were such as would sever a branch of green oak. Her eyes were black, her nose crooked and spread. Her body was scrawny, spotted and diseased. Her shins were bent. Her knees and ankles were thick, her shoulders broad, her nails were green. The hag's appearance was ugly.

'"You are horrible," said the lad. "Ay," said she. "Are you guarding the well?" said the lad. "Ay," said she.

---

[1] Cf. the smith Olc Acha in *Geineamain Cormaic* and *Cath Maige Mucrama* who foretold the birth of Cormac.

"May I fetch some water?" said the lad. "Ay," said she, "if you give me one kiss on the cheek." "No!" said he. "You shall have no water from me," said she. "I give my word," said he, "that I would rather die of thirst than kiss you." '

Fergus returned without water, and each of the brothers went in turn. Only Fiachra spoke temperately to the hag, and she promised that he would visit Tara. And that came true, says the story, for two of his descendants, Dá Thí and Ailill Molt, became kings of Ireland, but none of the descendants of the other three.

At last it was Niall's turn to go. When the hag asked him for a kiss, he consented and lay down with her. Then, when he looked upon her, she was as fair a girl as any in the world. She was as white as the last snow in a hollow. Her arms were full and queenly, her fingers long and slender, her legs straight and gleaming. She had two golden shoes on her bright little feet, and a precious purple cloak about her, held by a silver brooch. Her teeth were like pearls, her eyes large and queenly, her lips of Parthian red.

'"You are fair, woman," said the boy. "Ay," said she. "Who are you?" said the boy. "I am Sovranty," said she. And she said this:

"King of Tara, I am Sovranty. I shall tell you its virtue. Your seed shall be over every clan. There is good reason for what I say."'

She bade him return to his brothers with the water, and told him that he and his race would be kings of Ireland for ever, except for Dá Thí and Ailill Molt and one king from Munster, namely Brian Bórama. As he had seen her, horrible at first and beautiful in the end, so also is sovranty; for it is most often won by war and slaughter, but is glorious in the end. He was to give no water to his brothers until they granted him seniority over them, and that he might raise his weapon a hand's breadth above theirs. He returned with the water and exacted the promise as the maiden had taught him.

(18–19) The brothers returned to Tara, and as they put up their weapons, Niall placed his a hand's breadth higher than theirs. Eochu asked tidings of them, and Niall told their story. Mongfind inquired why it was not Brian, the eldest, that spoke. They answered that they had given seniority to Niall, and the first right to the kingship.[1] Sithchenn announced that they had forfeited it for ever, for Niall and his descendants would ever hold dominion over Ireland.

That came true, for none held the kingship of Ireland from Niall onward, save one of his children or descendants, down to Mael Shechlainn son of Domnall, except in revolt. And twenty-six kings of the Uí Néill of north and south held it, ten of the race of Conall and sixteen of the race of Eogan.

The death of Niall of the Nine Hostages in the territory of Gabrán, king of Scotland, while on an expedition in Britain, is told in an historical tract (ed. Meyer, *Otia Merseiana* ii 84–92), but has not been preserved in saga-form. Niall is alleged to have been slain by Eochu son of Énna Cennselach, but Meyer pointed out that this must be an error. Niall died in 405, and the death of Crimthann, another son of Énna Cennselach, is recorded in the Annals of Ulster *s.a.* 483. There is a short tale which forms a sequel to this tract in the manuscripts, entitled *Gein Branduib meic Echach 7 Aedáin meic Gabráin* ('The Birth-Tales of Brandub son of Eochu and of Aedán son of Gabrán') in which Aedán and Brandub are said to be in fact twin sons of this Eochu, who was exiled to Scotland for a time. Later Aedán, supposed to be a son of Gabrán, became king of Scotland, and invaded Ireland with an army of Scots and Britons. When he came against Brandub, who was then king of Leinster, his mother proved to him that he was her son, and Brandub's twin brother, by means of a grain of gold that she had hidden in his shoulder. Thus peace was made.[2]

[1] This would not exclude them or their heirs from succeeding upon his death under Irish law, s. MacNeill, *Celtic Ireland* 114.

[2] Ed. Meyer, ZCP 2, 134; another recension, ed. Best, *Loomis Studies* 381. The motif of the grain of gold recurs in the Feast of Dún na nGéd (*inf.* p. 63). Best points out that the story is pure fiction, as Brandub and Aedán belong to the close of the sixth century. Brandub, king of Leinster, was in fact a son of Muiredach Mór, eighth in descent from Cathaer Már (*ib.* 383); and Gabrán, king of Scotland, the father of Aedán, died in 559 (AU).

For the cycle of Brandub son of Eochu (*sic*) s. p. 49.

THE CYCLE OF RÓNÁN, KING OF LEINSTER
c. A.D. 600

RÓNÁN son of Colmán was king of Leinster (*Laigin*) in the early years of the seventh century. His death is recorded in the Annals of Ulster *s.a.* 623, and by the Four Masters under three dates, 610, 619, and 624. The *Chronicon Scotorum* gives alternative dates, 615 or 624.

AIDED MAELE FOTHARTAIG MAIC RÓNÁIN[1]
THE DEATH OF MAEL FOTHARTAIG SON OF RÓNÁN

Only one story about Rónán, king of Leinster, has come down to us, but it is worth attention. Kuno Meyer pointed out that it resembles the story of Phaedra and Hippolytus. It is mentioned in the list of sagas in LL and is also preserved in that manuscript (fcs. 271a47) and in H.3, 18 (p. 749). The story appears to be pure legend, for Echaid Iarlaithe, king of Dál Araide, whose daughter is here the wife of Rónán, died in 665 (AU), while Rónán died at least forty years earlier. Some confusion of names is possible, since Echaid (Eochu) is of frequent occurrence. The value of the story as history need not concern us here. It is well told, with perhaps more deliberate artistry than is common. The single motif is introduced in the first dialogue and repeated at once in the conversation between Mael Fothartaig and the queen. The tension is never relaxed.

The text is early Middle Irish, perhaps of the tenth century.

Ed. with translation, Meyer, RC 13, 368 (LL with variants from H); translation, Thurneysen, *Sagen aus dem alten Irland* 105. Numbers refer to the paragraphs of Meyer's edition.

(1) There was a famous king of Leinster, Rónán son of Aed;[2] and Eithne daughter of Cummascach son of Eogan of the Dési of Munster was his wife. She bore him a son, Mael Fothartaig son of Rónán. He was the most wonderful boy that ever was in Leinster. The crowd would gather round him in assemblies and games. He was the darling of the girls and young women.

---

[1] This is the title in the saga-list. In H there is no title, but the LL text bears the title *Fingal Rónáin* 'How Rónán slew his own kin'.

[2] Meyer points out that the story is told of Rónán son of Colmán in the genealogies, s. Rawl, B 502, 124 b 36, 50.

Eithne died and Rónán was for a long time without a wife.

'"Why have you not taken a wife?" said his son. "It were better for you to have a wife." "I am told," said Rónán, "that Echaid, king of Dunseverick in the north, has a lovely daughter." "You are no husband for a girl!" said the lad. "Will you not take a steady woman? I should think it fitter for you than a skittish girl."'

But Rónán was not to be dissuaded. He went north and brought the girl home with him; but Mael Fothartaig had gone on a visit to the south of Leinster. She asked where he was, for she had heard of his greatness, and asked that he be summoned to receive her.

'Then Mael Fothartaig comes and gives her a great welcome. "You shall have love," said the lad. "Whatever we have of treasures and wealth shall be yours for loving Rónán." "I am glad," said she, "that you care for me."'

(2) The queen sent her maid to solicit Mael Fothartaig, but the maid feared to speak. Once when he was playing chess with his two foster-brothers, Dond and Congal, the maid joined their game. She was trying to speak but did not dare, and she was blushing.

'The men noticed it. Mael Fothartaig went away. "What do you want to say," said Congal to the woman. "It is not I that want to speak," said she, "but Echaid's daughter wants to have Mael Fothartaig as her lover." "Do not say it, woman," said Congal. "You shall be killed if Mael Fothartaig hears it. But I shall speak to him for yourself, if you wish it."'

The queen consented to this, and bade the maid use her advantage to speak for her. The maid slept with Mael Fothartaig, and the queen soon suspected that she was keeping him for herself, and threatened to kill her. She told Mael Fothartaig of the queen's desire. He was angry, and said that though he should be burnt to ashes he would not go to Rónán's wife. He would go away so as to avoid her.

(3) Mael Fothartaig went to Scotland accompanied by fifty warriors, and he was welcomed by the king. There he excelled in hunting and in battle. His hounds Doilín and Daithlenn were swifter than all the king's hounds. But the Men of Leinster

threatened to kill Rónán, their king, unless Mael Fothartaig returned. He heard that and went back to Ireland. He landed at Dunseverick and was made welcome. 'It is bad of you that you have not slept with my daughter,' says Echaid. 'It was for you I gave her and not for that old churl!' 'That is bad indeed,' said Mael Fothartaig.

He came to Leinster and was made welcome, and the queen's maid again shared his bed. Echaid's daughter again threatened her life, if she did not persuade him to become her lover. Mael Fothartaig turned to Congal for advice, and Congal promised to cure the queen of her passion if he got a reward. Mael Fothartaig offered his horse and bridle and his cloak; but Congal would have the two precious hounds, and they were promised him. Congal sent Mael Fothartaig out hunting and sent a message to the queen that she might go to a tryst with him. She could hardly wait for the morning. In the morning she and her maid set out for the trysting-place. They met with Congal.

'"Whither away, harlot?" said he. "You do ill to travel alone, unless it be to meet a man. Go home, and bad luck go with you!" He went with her to her house.

They saw her coming again. "Nay," said Congal, "you will bring shame on the king of Leinster, you wicked woman. If I see you again, I shall bring your head and fix it on a stake in Rónán's presence, as that of a wicked woman who shamed him in ditches and brakes, going alone to tryst with a lad!" He took a horse-whip to her and left her in the house. "I shall bring blood into your mouth," said she.'

(4) Rónán came in. Mael Fothartaig's companions came in before him, and Rónán asked where he was, and regretted his absence. The queen complained that Rónán was always talking of his son.

'"It is right to speak of him," said Rónán, "for there is not in Ireland a son more faithful to his father. For his zeal for us both, man and wife, at Áth Cliath and Clár Daire Mór and Droichet Cairpri[1] is as great as though it were his own life that were at stake, all for my sake, so that you and I may have comfort, wife."

---

[1] Perhaps the limits of Rónán's territory.

'"He does not get from me the comfort he desires," said she, "which is to come in to me in your despite. I will put up with him no longer. Three times since morning Congal has taken me to him, and it went hard that I escaped him."

'"A curse on your lips, wicked woman!" said Rónán. "You lie!"

'"You shall see proof of it now," said she. "I shall make a half-quatrain to see whether it will fit what he makes."

'He used to do that every night to please her. He would make a half-quatrain, and she would make the other half.[1]

'Then he came in and was drying his legs at the fire, and Congal was beside him. Mael Fothartaig's jester, Mac Glas, was playing on the floor. Then he said, for the day was cold:

"It is cold against the wind
for him who herds the cows of the slope."

'"Listen to this, Rónán!" said she. "Say that again," said she.

"It is cold against the wind
for him who herds the cows of the slope." '

'She said:

"It is a vain herding
without cows, without one you love."

(That is: "I did not come, and you did not bring home the cows.")

'"It is true, then," said Rónán. There was a warrior beside Rónán, Aedán son of Fiachna Lára. "Aedán," said he, "a spear into Mael Fothartaig, and strike Congal too!" Since his back was towards them as he faced the fire, Aedán thrust the spear into him and its head went through him and fixed him to his seat. As Congal rose, Aedán thrust a spear into him which pierced his heart. The fool jumped away. Aedán cast a spear after him which tore out his bowels.

'"Enough have you played against the men, Aedán!" said Mael Fothartaig from where he sat.

'"You were lucky indeed," said Rónán, "to find no other woman to entreat but my wife!"

[1] This form of entertainment is illustrated in *Tromdám Guaire* 1180–1211 (*inf.*, p. 96). It persisted into modern times, s. Douglas Hyde, *Amhráin Chúige Chonnacht: An Leathrann.*

'"That is a sad deception that has been put upon you, Rónán," said the lad, "to kill your only son unjustly. By your majesty and by the tryst to which I go, the tryst of death, I no more thought of lying with her than I would lie with my mother. But she has been soliciting me since she came to this country, and three times to-day Congal brought her back to keep her from me. Congal did not deserve his death."

'A raven was gathering the bowels of the jester on to the front bridge. The churls were laughing. Mael Fothartaig was ashamed. He said:

> "Mac Glas,
>   gather in your bowels:
>   although you know no shame
>   the churls are mocking you."'

'Then the three died. They were brought into a separate house. Rónán went and stayed by the head of his son for three days and three nights.'

His lamentation for his son has the eloquence of restraint:

> '"It is cold against the wind
> for him who herds the cows of the slope:
> it is a vain herding
> without cows, without one you love.
>
> The wind is cold
> in front of the warrior's house:
> dear were the warriors
> who used to be between me and the wind.
>
> Sleep, daughter of Echaid.
> The wind is fierce.
> Woe is me that Mael Fothartaig
> was slain for the guilt of a lustful woman.
>
> Sleep, daughter of Echaid.
> I have no comfort though you sleep not,
> seeing Mael Fothartaig
> in his bloody shroud."'

But Dond, Congal's brother and foster-brother to Mael Fothartaig, went with twenty horsemen to Dunseverick; and lured forth Echaid to the boundary of his territory by pretend-

ing that Mael Fothartaig had eloped with his daughter and was
on his way there. They killed Echaid and his wife and son, and
brought back their heads, and threw them upon the queen's
breast. She arose and threw herself on her knife.

'Then Rónán said:

"Echaid has got a shroud
after being in a fine mantle;
the grief that is upon Dún Ais
is also upon Dunseverick.

Give food and drink
to Mael Fothartaig's hound,
the hound of a man who would give food
to him from whom he bought.[1]

It is said to me that Daithlenn suffers
with her ribs spare through her sides:
I have no grievance against her,
it is not she who has betrayed my dear ones.

Doiléne
served me well:
her head is in the lap of everyone in turn
seeking one whom she will not find.

The men, the youths, the horses
that were around Mael Fothartaig,
they were not eager for protection
in the lifetime of their lord.

.   .   .   .

My son, Mael Fothartaig,
whose dwelling was the tall wood,
neither kings nor princes
would part from him without respect.

My son, Mael Fothartaig,
he was the hound around whom the pack would close,
the tall white flashing salmon,
he has found a cold dwelling."'

---

[1] In Ireland to-day it is the seller who must make a gift, s. E. Estyn Evans,
Irish Heritage 162; but he mistakenly says that the seller receives the 'luck-
money'. For the buyer to make a gift as here would be an act of great
generosity.

The two sons of Mael Fothartaig pursued the man who had killed him, and killed him in revenge.

'Then Rónán said:

"It is a great matter
for the son of a churl to kill the son of a king:
that was clear on the day of his death
to Aedán son of Fiachna Lára."

'After that the fight was brought close to him, up to the door of the house. Then he said:

"This fighting outside,
I await it without Mael Fothartaig:
against this last fight
an old champion cannot stand."

'With that, the blood came from his mouth and he died at once. That is how Rónán slew his son.'

THE CYCLE OF MONGÁN SON OF FIACHNA AND BRANDUB SON OF EOCHU, A.D. 624

BRANDUB son of Eochu, king of Leinster, was twin-brother to Aedán son of Gabrán, king of Scotland, according to an anecdote edited by Kuno Meyer, ZCP 2, 134–7.[1] The wife of Eochu brought forth two boys and the wife of Gabrán two girls on the same night, while Eochu was in exile in Scotland. And Feidelm, wife of Eochu, gave one of her sons in exchange for one of the girls; but she put a grain of gold in his shoulder by which she might identify him afterwards. Eochu and his wife returned to Ireland with their children; and their son Brandub became king of Leinster, tenth in descent from Cathaer Már. Later when Aedán came to make war upon Leinster his mother identified him and reconciled him to his brother.

Mongán was begotten by Manannán Mac Lir upon the wife of Fiachna while he was fighting the king of Lochlann,[2] and the child, according to one story, was a reincarnation of Find Mac Cumaill.[3] The death of Brandub is recorded in the Annals of Ulster *s.a.* 604, and that of Mongán *s.a.* 624.

Three anecdotes about Mongán were edited by Meyer in an Appendix to the *Voyage of Bran*, and Vernam Hull has since published them from a manuscript not consulted by Meyer.[4] A fourth has been edited by Eleanor Knott.[5] He also figures in the anecdote about St. Colum Cille edited by Paul Grosjean from the Book of Lecan.[6] There is one longer tale in Meyer's collection which deserves notice here.

COMPERT MONGÁIN 7 SERC DUIBE LACHA DO MONGÁN

THE BIRTH OF MONGÁN AND HIS LOVE FOR DUB LACHA

The text is preserved in the Book of Fermoy (p. 131 = f 85a, 15th century)[7] and the language is early Modern Irish, perhaps not much older than the manuscript. A good modern recension, in

[1] *v. sup.*, p. 41.
[2] Or with Aedán son of Gabrán against the Saxons, according to a variant tradition, s. Kuno Meyer and Alfred Nutt, *Voyage of Bran* i 44 and 72.
[3] *Op. cit.* i 49. Nutt discusses the Celtic doctrine of re-birth in vol. ii.
[4] ZCP 18, 414–19.   [5] *Ériu* 8, 155–60.
[6] RC 49, 185. Read 'Book of Lecan fcs. 193b8' as the source of the text.
[7] Cat. Ir. MSS. R.I.A. p. 3092.

which the humour is well developed, has been edited by Séamas Ó Duilearga[1] from a nineteenth-century manuscript in the possession of Douglas Hyde. The Fermoy recension is summarized here.[2]

Ed. with translation, Meyer, *Voyage of Bran* i 58–84.

(1) Fiachna the Fair son of Baetán set out from Ireland and came to Lochlann where Eolgarg Mór son of Magar was king. He was received with honour. Eolgarg fell sick, and his leeches told him that the only cure for him was the flesh of a white cow with red ears.[3] The only such cow to be found was the cow of a certain black hag. She refused to exchange it for another, but accepted a promise of four cows on condition that Fiachna was the surety. Fiachna was summoned back to Ireland and became king of Ulster.

(2) A year later the black hag appeared at the king's fort in Ulster to claim the performance of his guarantee, for Eolgarg had denied her payment. Fiachna offered her four score cows for the four that were due, but she would accept nothing less than the enforcement of her claim against Eolgarg.

(3–6) Fiachna raised an army and invaded Lochlann. Eolgarg opposed him, and he loosed a flock of venomous sheep against the men of Ireland which killed three hundred warriors each day for three days. Fiachna resolved to fight the sheep himself. But as he was about to take his weapons, a tall warrior approached him. The warrior wore a green cloak with a brooch of silver, a circlet of gold on his head, and golden sandals. He offered to ward off the sheep on condition that he might spend a night with Fiachna's wife in Ireland, and demanded the king's ring as a token. Fiachna replied that he would not suffer the death of a single one of his men if it might be so averted. The warrior foretold the birth of a glorious child from his meeting with the wife of Fiachna, and promised to come to her in the likeness of Fiachna so that she should not be put to shame. He declared that he was Manannán Mac Lir, and promised victory to Fiachna. He then took from his cloak a fierce dog and promised that it would kill the sheep and three hundred of the men of Lochlann. So it fell out, and Fiachna seized the kingship of Lochlann and of the Saxons and the Britons. He compen-

---

[1] ZCP 17, 347–70.

[2] James Stephens tells the story in his *Irish Fairy Tales*, p. 259.

[3] Bergin has recently called attention to the survival in England of herds of white cattle with red ears in a wild state, the purest being the Chillingham herd in Northumberland, *Ériu* 15, 170.

sated the hag with seven castles and the land belonging to them, and a hundred cattle of each kind.

Fiachna returned to Ireland and found his wife pregnant. In due time she bore a son, Mongán; and on the same night the wife of Fiachna's servant, An Damh, bore a son who was called Mac an Daimh. They were christened together. Fiachna the Black reigned jointly with Fiachna the Fair,[1] and his wife bore a daughter that same night. She was named Dubh Lacha; and Mongán and Dubh Lacha were betrothed. When Mongán was three days old, Manannán came and took him to the Land of Promise to rear him there till he should be twelve years of age. Then Fiachna the Fair was slain by Fiachna the Black, who seized the kingship of Ulster by force. The men of Ulster wished Mongán to be brought back, but he was only six years old; and Manannán did not restore him to them till he was sixteen. Then peace was made between the men of Ulster and Fiachna the Black. Mongán was given half the kingdom of Ulster and Dubh Lacha as his wife in compensation for his father's death.

(7–9) Manannán came disguised as a cleric and incited Mongán to avenge his father. Mongán set out and slew Fiachna;[2] and he, in turn, became king of Ulster. He then went on a circuit of Ireland and came to Leinster. Brandubh son of Eochu was then king, and he made Mongán welcome. Brandubh had fifty white cows with red ears, and a white calf with every cow, and Mongán desired to have them. The king of Leinster observed that, and offered him the cows on condition of 'friendship without refusal'. The two kings bound each other to this agreement, and Mongán returned home with the cows. Soon he saw a host approaching. It was Brandubh and his retinue. Mongán asked him his quest, and promised that if it was anything in Ulster he should have it. Brandubh demanded Dubh Lacha.

---

[1] Fiachna the Black was king of Dál Fiatach according to the *Annals of the Four Masters* A.D. 597 and 622. His death is recorded AU 626. Fiachna the Fair (also called Fiachna Lurgan) was king of Dál Araide according to a list of kings in the Book of Leinster, and king of Ulster according to another list (LL fcs. 41c11, e 12). Battles between the two Fiachnas are recorded AU 601 and 625. In the first Fiachna the Fair was the victor: the second was won by Fiachna the Black, and Fiachna the Fair was slain. Fiachna the Black was killed in a battle against Dál Riada in the following year. The warfare between the two Fiachnas is described in the Fragmentary Annals published by O'Grady, SG ii 424–8.

[2] This conflicts with the tradition of the Annals noted above, cf. FM 624.

(10–12) 'I have never heard of anyone giving away his wife,' said Mongán. 'Though you have not heard of it,' said Dubh Lacha, 'do so, for honour is more lasting than life.' Mongán was angry, but he surrendered his wife to Brandubh. Dubh Lacha, however, exacted a promise from Brandubh that he should not become her husband for a year. Brandubh and Dubh Lacha went away into Leinster, and Mongán wasted away for love of his wife. But his servant's wife, who was Dubh Lacha's maid, had gone with her mistress, and Mac an Daimh was lonely too. One day he came to Mongán and reproached him for having learned nothing from Manannán in the Land of Promise save how to eat and amuse himself; and he complained that he had lost his wife through Mongán's fault. Mongán bade him fetch from a secret cave a basket in which there was a sod of earth from Scotland and a sod from Ireland. He would go to Leinster standing on these two sods, Mac an Daimh carrying the basket on his back, so as to confuse the druids of Brandubh. When the king asked them for news of him, they would say that he had one foot in Ireland and the other in Scotland,[1] and Brandubh would not then expect him.

(13–16) They travelled in this way, and as they came into Leinster they met the king on his way to the fair of Mag Life. Then they met Tibraide and another monk, chanting the Office, book in hand. Mongán made a river through the plain in front of Tibraide with a bridge across it.[2] Tibraide wondered at that, for no river had been seen there before, but he entered upon the bridge to cross over. The bridge fell under the monks, and Mongán snatched the gospel book from Tibraide's hand as he fell. He decided not to let them drown, but that they should be carried a mile down the stream. Mongán took the form of Tibraide and gave Mac an Daimh the form of the other monk, and so they proceeded into the king's presence. He welcomed them and bade them go before him to his fort where the wife of the king of Ulster would receive them and would be glad to make her confession to Tibraide. They went to the fort. Dubh Lacha recognized Mongán, and when the house had been

---

[1] This answer would suggest that he was in the territory of Dál Riada, which extended across the sea.
[2] He had acquired in the Land of Promise some of the power of his father and fosterer Manannán.

cleared so that the queen might confess to the cleric, Mongán and Mac an Daimh took their wives to bed.

(17) 'Then they heard a knocking at the door, and it was Tibraide with a company of three times nine. The door-keepers said; "We never saw a year in which Tibraides were more plentiful than this year. You have a Tibraide within and a Tibraide without." "That is true," said Mongán. "It is Mongán who has come disguised as myself. And go out," said he, "and I grant you absolution if you will kill those monks, for they are Mongán's followers disguised as monks." And the men went out and killed those monks, and twice nine of them were slain by them. And the king of Leinster met the sur-vivors and asked them why they fled. "Mongán," they said, "has come disguised as Tibraide, and Tibraide is in the place." The king bade his men attack them, and Tibraide escaped to the church of Cill Chamáin, and none of the nine got away without a hurt.'

(18) 'And the king of Leinster came to his house, and Mongán then departed. And the king of Leinster asked: "Where is Tibraide?" said he. "It was not Tibraide," said the girl, "but Mongán, for you should hear of it anyway." "Were you with Mongán, girl?" said he. "I was," said she, "for he has the better claim upon me." "Send for Tibraide!" said the king of Leinster. "For it is an evil chance that we have killed his people." And Tibraide was brought to him. And Mongán went to his house, and stayed for three months with-out returning, and for that time he was in a wasting sickness.'

(19–21) Mac an Daimh again complained to Mongán that he was being separated from his wife through Mongán's fault; and Mongán bade him go to Ráth Deiscirt mBregh where Dubh Lacha was, to seek tidings of her, for he was too weak to go himself. Dubh Lacha told him that Brandubh was away on a circuit of Leinster so that she had an opportunity to escape, and that Mongán should come to her. He came then, and, as he sat playing chess with Dubh Lacha, she bared her breasts before him; and when he saw her full soft white breasts and the bright cleft between them, he longed for her, and Dubh Lacha was aware of it. At that moment the king of Leinster came to the gate with his followers and was admitted. Dubh Lacha

confessed that Mongán had been with her. The king asked her a
favour, and she answered that she would refuse him nothing,
provided he did not make her his wife till the year was up. He
asked her to let him know whenever Mongán should come into
her mind, for whenever he should set out towards Leinster she
would think of him.

Three months later Mongán came again, and he was in her
thoughts.[1] The hosts of the fort came out and Mongán turned
back and went home; and again he was in a wasting sickness.
His people offered to go with him into Leinster to fight for the
woman, but Mongán would not suffer the death of a single man
on account of his own folly.

(22) When a year had passed, the chiefs of Leinster assembled
for the wedding of Dubh Lacha. Mongán and Mac an Daimh
came from Ulster and arrived on the lawn outside the fort.
Mac an Daimh asked in what disguise they should approach.
Just then they saw Cuimne, the Hag of the Mill, with a cur on
a leash and a nag that used to draw corn to the mill and deliver
the meal. Mongán summoned her and changed her with a touch
of his magic wand into a beautiful girl in the likeness of Íbhell
of the Bright Cheeks, daughter of the king of Munster. He
changed the cur into a pretty lap dog that fitted on the palm
of her hand, with a silver chain around his neck, and a little
gold bell, and the nag into a shining palfrey with a gilt saddle
set with precious stones. He himself took the form of Áedh,
son of the king of Connacht, with Mac an Daimh as his servant,
and thus they approached the fort.

(24–7) The king of Leinster welcomed them, and when they
were seated in the banquet-hall, Mongán put a love-charm in
the cheeks of the hag so that the king was filled with love for
her. He sent a message to her that he loved her, and that a
king was better than a prince. Mongán observed that and bade
the hag reply that she would acknowledge gifts as proof of love.
The king gave her his cup. His household protested, saying:
'Do not give your treasures to the wife of the king of Connacht!'
But he said: 'The woman and my treasures shall be mine.' He
gave her a magic belt which protected the wearer against sickness. But Mac an Daimh took from her each gift that she

---

[1] We must understand that Dubh Lacha kept her promise and announced
his approach.

received during the night. At last the king offered Dubh Lacha
to Mongán in exchange for the hag, and Mongán, with a great
show of anger, consented. He gave the hag three kisses as she
left him, lest they should suspect that he was not unwilling to
lose her. The feast went on until all were drunk.

(28) Then Mac an Daimh arose and said: 'It is a great shame
that there is none to serve a drink to the son of the king of
Connacht.' Since there was no reply, they took the two swiftest
horses in the fort, and with their wives behind them, they set
out for home. Next morning when the household awoke, they
saw the hag in the king's bed, and the dog and the nag in their
true form, and they laughed aloud. The king awoke and saw
the hag beside him. 'Are you Greyhaired Cuimne of the Mill?'
he said. 'Ay,' said she. 'Pity that I should have slept with
thee, Cuimne.'

The Battle of Belach Dúin Bolg which is preserved in YBL
(fcs. 207b37) belongs also to the Cycle of Brandub, but it is still
unedited. The tale has been incorporated in the history of the
Bórama (inf. pp. 106–11). Brandub figures also in the Life of
St. Maedóc of Ferns, where the events of the battle are told,
Lives of Irish Saints, ii. 223–4. The death of Brandub by the
hand of Saran is told ib. 182. There is a legend about his death
and miraculous restoration to life by the aid of St. Colum Cille
in the Book of Lecan (fcs. 193b8) which Reeves published in
translation, *Vita Sancti Columbae*, 205, note a. It appears in
Manus O'Donnell's *Life of Colum Cille* (ed. O'Kelleher and
Schoepperle), 213–15.

THE CYCLE OF DOMNALL SON OF AED SON OF AINMIRE, A.D. 628–42

THIS is one of the greatest of the historical cycles. It comprises three famous tales, and centres around an heroic struggle for the high kingship which is a matter of history. The battle of Moira[1] was fought in 637 between Domnall son of Aed, king of Ireland, and Domnall Brecc, king of Dál Riada, the Irish kingdom in Scotland, which at that time included a small territory in north-east Ireland. The occasion of the battle was a feud between the Irish king and Congal Caech, king of the Ulaid. Congal had killed Suibne Menn, king of Ireland, whom Domnall succeeded. Congal then opposed Domnall and was defeated at Dún Cethirn. He fled to Scotland, and the Scottish Domnall took up his cause and sent an army to Ireland. The king of Ireland was victorious, and one result of the battle seems to have been the loss to the Scottish kingdom of its Irish territory.[2] It must have been an event of historic importance, for it became the subject of legendary traditions. In the preface to an old law-tract is said: 'The three virtues of that battle are the defeat of Congal Cloen in his falsehood by Domnall in his truth, and that Suibne the Madman became mad, and that the brain of forgetfulness was taken out of the head of Cennfaelad. And the virtue is not in Suibne's becoming mad, but in all the stories and poems he left after him in Ireland. And the virtue is not that the brain of forgetfulness was taken out of the head of Cennfaelad, but in all the book-learning that he left after him in Ireland.'[3] Moreover, three sagas about this general theme have been preserved. The first, 'The Feast of Dún na nGéd', leads up to the battle; the second is 'The Battle of Moira'; the third, 'The Frenzy of Sweeny', tells the adventures of the famous madman.

[1] Moira, Co. Down, near Lurgan.

[2] s. Tigernach, RC 17, 181; 183–4; MacNeill, *Phases of Irish History* 199–200; Marstrander, *Ériu* 5, 226–7.

[3] AL iii 88. The text goes on to say that, as a result of this wound, Cennfaelad remembered everything he heard recited in the three schools of Latin, Law and Poetry that he afterwards attended. He then recorded all this learning in a book. For a variant account of the three virtues of the battle s. *inf.*, p. 64. In the version quoted by O'Donovan, MR² 280, footnote, there is an alternative including as a fourth virtue the escape of Dub Diad to Scotland. All four virtues of the battle are mentioned in *Auraicept na nÉces* 72–8.

FLED DÚIN NA NGÉD
THE FEAST OF DÚN NA NGÉD

The text is preserved in a gathering of YBL written in 1401 (fcs. 319a1),[1] and in other manuscripts. It is earlier in style than the LL Táin, and the language preserves some old forms. I should place the extant recension in the eleventh century. It contains echoes of *Cath Maige Mucrama*: a woman's curse is here too the cause of the tragedy; Congal flees to Scotland and returns with an army of Scots and Britons, as does Lugaid Mac Con; Congal, in telling of the death of Suibne Menn, uses a phrase apparently borrowed from the earlier story, saying that the pillar stone behind the slain man answered the blow; Congal, like Lugaid, ties his men in pairs lest they flee.

Ed. with translation from YBL, O'Donovan, *The Banquet of Dún na nGédh and the Battle of Mag Rath*, Dublin, Irish Archaeological Society, 1842; text (YBL with variant readings), Marstrander, *Skrifter Vidensk-Selsk. i Christiania 1909, II Hist. Fil. Kl. no. 6*.

'There was once a famous king of Ireland, Domnall son of Aed son of Ainmire son of Sédna son of Fergus Long-Head son of Conall Gulban son of Niall of the Nine Hostages, of the race of Conn of the Hundred Battles and Úgaine Már. For it was Úgaine Már who took pledges by the sun and moon and sea and dew and light and by all the elements visible and invisible and every element in heaven and on earth that the kingship of Ireland should belong to his children for ever. And Tuathal Techtmar son of Fiacha Finnola took the same pledges, after the manner of his ancestor Úgaine Már; and if any should contest against his children for the kingship of Ireland in spite of those pledges and the elements by which he had bound them, that the lawful right to Tara with its supporting families and the ancient communities of Tara and Meath should still belong to his children for ever; and though some one of the children of Úgaine or Tuathal should consent to grant the kingship to someone else, nonetheless that king shall have no right to enter Tara unless he give a territory equally established to the children of Úgaine Már and Tuathal Techtmar for as long as he shall be king over them, and when that king shall die, Tara shall belong to the children of

[1] s. Abbott and Gwynn, *Catalogue of Irish Manuscripts in Trinity College, Dublin, 344.*

Ugaine, as Ugaine himself bound upon the men of Ireland
when he took hostages from Ireland and Scotland and as far
as Brittany in the east. But Tara was cursed by Ruadán of
Lothra and by the twelve apostles of Ireland and all the
saints of Ireland.[1] And whosoever took the kingship it was
not lucky for him to dwell at Tara after it had been cursed;
but whatever place seemed most venerable and most pleasant
to the king who became king of Ireland, there his seat and
dwelling used to be, as indeed Domnall son of Áed established
his seat at Dún na nGéd on the bank of the Boyne. And he
designed seven great ramparts about that fort after the
manner of Tara of the Kings, and he designed even the houses
of the fort after the manner of the houses of Tara: namely,
the great Central Hall where the king himself used to abide,
with kings and queens and ollams, and all that were best in
every art; and the Hall of Munster and the Hall of Leinster
and the Banquet-Hall of Connacht and the Assembly-Hall
of Ulster and the Prison of the Hostages and the Star of the
Poets and the Palace of the Single Pillar (which Cormac son
of Art first made for his daughter) and all the other houses.'

Domnall saw one night in a dream that a whelp that he had
reared on his own knee went from him raging and gathered the
packs of Ireland, Scotland, the Saxons and the Britons against
Ireland. The dogs fought seven battles against him and the
men of Ireland, and were defeated in the seventh battle, and
his own dog was killed in that last battle. Domnall leaped naked
from the bed on to the floor. The queen put her arms around
his neck and bade him stay beside her and not be frightened
by a dream, when the people of Conall and of Eogan and of
Oriel, and the Clann Colmáin and the race of Aed Sláine and
the four families of Tara were gathered around him. The king
went back to bed, but refused to tell his dream till he should
consult his brother, Mael Chaba the cleric, the best interpreter
of dreams in Ireland.

Mael Chaba had renounced the kingship of Ireland for the
love of God and retired to a hermitage at Druim Dilair where
he dwelt with a hundred monks and ten women for the sacrifice

[1] The story of the cursing of Tara (*Betha Ruaddin*) is preserved in the
Book of Fermoy (f. 93a) and was edited by O'Grady, SG i 66 = ii 70. Cf.
MacNeill, *Phases of Irish History* 233.

of the Mass and the recital of the Office. The king told him his
dream, and Mael Chaba explained it, for it had long since been
foretold. A whelp in a dream means a king's son. The king had
two fosterlings, Cobthach Caem son of Ragallach, and Congal
Claen son of Scannlán of the Broad Shield. Now Ragallach was
king of Connacht, and Congal was himself king of Ulster.
Either of the two would go into revolt and bring marauders
from Scotland and from the Franks, Saxons and Britons to
Ireland. Seven battles would be fought, and in the seventh
battle the rebellious fosterson would fall. The hermit advised
that the king should give a feast for the men of Ireland and
take hostages from each province, and that these two fostersons
should be held captive for a year, for the harm goes out of every
dream in a year, and that they should then be dismissed with
gifts. The king replied that he would rather depart out of
Ireland than use treachery against his own fostersons, and
moreover that though all the world should oppose him Congal
would never oppose him. In a short poem the dialogue of the
king and the hermit is repeated.

The king went home and prepared a feast for his inauguration.[1] He sent out stewards to procure all the goose-eggs they
could find, for he was eager that nothing should be lacking to
the feast. It was not easy to get them. The stewards travelled
through Meath and came at last upon a hut occupied by a holy
woman, where they found a basin full of goose-eggs. They
seized the eggs in spite of the woman's protest. She told them
the hut was the hermitage of a saint whose practice it was to
stand all day in the river Boyne up to his armpits reciting the
psalms, and in the evening to sup of an egg and a half with four
sprigs of cress from the Boyne. They made no answer, but carried off the eggs. Great evil came of this, for Ireland has since
known no peace. When the holy man returned, he was angry
and laid his heaviest curse on the feast that was being prepared.

A hideous couple arrived at the palace. Their limbs were
huge, their shins sharp as a razor, the feet reversed; if a bushel
of apples were thrown on their heads, not an apple would fall
to the ground, but each would be impaled upon each single

---

[1] The Irish term is *fled baindsi* 'wedding-feast', the original belief being
that the king was espoused to the goddess Ériu, s. O'Rahilly *Ériu* 14, 14, and
cf. *sup.*, pp. 11, 38.

hair; their bodies were black as coal, their eyes white as snow; the woman had a beard and the man had none.[1] Between them they carried a tub of goose-eggs. They announced that they were guests coming to the feast and bringing their share. The king made them welcome, and food for a hundred men was set before them. The man alone devoured it. Food for a hundred was again set down, and the woman alone devoured it and asked for more. The same ration was given them, and this time they shared it. 'Give us food,' they said, 'if you have it.' But the steward refused, until the men of Ireland should come to the feast. They replied that evil would come of their being first to partake of the feast, for they were of the host of Hell, and the devils were preparing trouble for the company. They leaped away and vanished.

'The kings of the provinces were bidden to that feast, with their petty kings and chiefs and lords and soldiers and artists ordinary and extraordinary. The kings of the provinces of Ireland at that time were: Congal Claen son of Scannlán, king of Ulster, Crimthann son of Aed Cerr, king of Leinster, Mael Dúin son of Aed Bennán, king of Munster, and his brother Illann son of Aed Bennán, king of South Munster, and Ragallach son of Uada, king of Connacht. And Domnall son of Aed was himself High King of Ireland over them all.'[2]

When all were assembled, Domnall welcomed them and asked Congal to go into the banquet-hall and appraise the feast. Congal went in and beheld the food and wine and ale, and his eye rested upon the goose-eggs, and he ate a bite from one of them and drank afterwards. He came out and declared that though the men of Ireland should stay four months they would have enough to eat and drink. The king then went in and he was told of the saint's curse. He asked who had eaten of the

---

[1] Cf. the description of the strange visitor to Da Derga's Hostel, RC 22, 57.

[2] This list of provincial kings is quoted for its historical interest. Here, as at pp. 31 and 104, two kingdoms of Munster are distinguished, and the territory of the High King is not reckoned. This is the division reported by Giraldus Cambrensis, *Top. Hib.* I vii. The traditional division, according to Thurneysen, was Ulster, Leinster, Connacht, Munster, and Meath, *Heldensage* 75–6. For the historical period the Synchronisms list provincial kings of Scotland, Ulster, Leinster, Ossory (only for a period), Munster, and Connacht, ZCP 19, 81–99. MacNeill discusses the ancient division, and recognizes a later division into seven provincial kingdoms, *Phases of Irish History* 102–13.

egg, for he knew that the first man to partake of the feast after it had been cursed would be the man who would oppose him. They told him that it was his own fosterson, Congal; and the king was sad, for he knew that Congal had often shown folly and wickedness.

The twelve apostles of Ireland were summoned to bless the feast and remove the curse. They were Findén of Moville and Findén of Clonard and Colum Cille and Colm son of Crimthann, Ciarán of Clonmacnoise, Caindech son of Ua Daland, Comgall of Bangor, Brendan son of Findlug and Brendan of Birr, Ruadán of Lothra, Nindid the Pious, Mo Bhí Clárainech and Mo Laise son of Nat Fraech.[1] They all blessed the feast, but Congal had already partaken of it, and that evil they could not undo.

The custom was that when a king of the Southern Uí Néill was High King the king of Connacht should be at his right hand, and when a king of the Northern Uí Néill was High King the king of Ulster on his right and the king of Connacht on his left. But on this occasion the king of the nine cantreds of Oriel sat beside Domnall, from which great harm resulted. Food and drink were served until all were merry, and a goose-egg on a silver dish was placed before each king. The silver dish was changed to wood, and the goose-egg to a hen-egg, after they had been placed before Congal Claen. His people were outraged at this, and one of the Ulster lords complained of the double insult, for Congal had also been deprived of his seat at the High King's right hand. Congal would not at first pay heed, for he expected no dishonour in his foster-father's house. The same man spoke again, and his words are given in a short poem.

This time Congal was seized with rage, and the fury Tesiphone entered into his heart to prompt him to evil. The king's steward tried to restrain him and was cut down in the presence of the assembled guests. Then Congal proceeded to recite his grievances. Domnall had sought the friendship of Ulster and received Congal into fosterage, but had sent back to Ulster the nurse who brought the child, and entrusted him to a woman of his

[1] All of these saints (thirteen names occur) died in the sixth century, and could not have been present, but the list is of interest. A list of thirteen saints present at the Assembly of Druim Cett, which includes many of these names, occurs in *Tromddm Guaire* 124–9 (s. p. 92), and a similar list *ibid.* 1290–5 (p. 98). Thurneysen traces it to the introduction to the commentary on *Amra Choluimb Chille* (*Heldensage* 258, note 1), but I have not found it there.

own people. Through this woman's neglect Congal had been stung in the eye by a bee so that he squinted: whence his name Congal Claen ('Crooked'). Then Domnall had been forced to flee to Scotland by Suibne Menn, who was High King at that time, and had taken Congal with him. They returned to Ireland, and Domnall had encouraged Congal to kill Suibne, promising him security in his possessions when he Domnall should be High King. Congal had stolen upon Suibne as he was playing chess and thrust his spear through him so that the stone against which he sat answered the spear. As he was dying, the king hurled a chessman at Congal and destroyed his squinting eye. He was Congal Claen already, and after that he was Congal Caech ('One-Eyed'). Domnall became High King, and Congal, on his father's death, came to be confirmed in the kingship of Ulster as had been promised him; but the promise was not fulfilled. Tyrone, Tyrconnell and the nine cantreds of Oriel had been taken from him, and Oriel given to Maelodar Macha who now sat at the right hand of the High King in Congal's place. Maelodar got a goose-egg on a dish of silver, and he a hen-egg on a dish of wood.

After this recital Congal vowed to avenge his wrongs and went out, followed by the men of Ulster. Domnall first sent the holy men after Congal to persuade him to return to the feast and accept satisfaction, but he threatened to kill them. Then the poets were sent, and he received them with gifts, but would accept no satisfaction but war. He went to the house of Cellach, his father's brother, and told his story. Cellach, who had been a great warrior, was now deaf and helpless with age, but he girded on his sword and said: 'I swear if you had accepted any satisfaction from the king but war, the men of Ulster could not prevent me from running this sword through your heart, for it is not the custom of Ulster to accept satisfaction before the battle until they have avenged their wrongs. And I have seven good sons, and they will go with you into the battle, and I would go myself if I could. They shall not boast over Ulster while I live.' In a spirited poem he incites his nephew to vengeance.

Congal crossed the sea to Scotland to seek the aid of his grandfather, Echaid the Yellow son of Aedán, king of Scotland, who dwelt at Dún Monaid. His mother was a daughter of

Echaid, and Echaid's wife was a daughter of Echaid Aingces, king of the Britons. Echaid told Congal that he had promised Domnall, when he was in exile in Scotland, never to oppose him, but that his four sons would join in an expedition against Ireland. A council was held, and the king's chief druid, Dub Diad, and the other druids were petitioned to give them a sign whether the expedition would prosper. The druids counselled against it, and Echaid advised Congal to go to the king of the Britons and invoke his aid.

While the Britons were in council with Congal, a strange warrior came up to the place where they were, and sat on the king's right hand, between him and Congal. The others asked him why he sat there, and he answered that no seat had been offered him and that that was the best he could find. The king laughed and said he had done right. They asked him for news, and he gave them the news of all the world. They asked his name and race, but he refused to answer.

The crowd dispersed into the fort, leaving the warrior alone on the mound where the council had been held. The king's poet came up and conversed with him. Then heavy sleet and snow began to fall, and the warrior sheltered the poet with his shield, and laid down his weapons in the snow. The poet bade him come to his house for the night, and the warrior went along with him.

The king's messenger came to summon the poet, and they went to the fort. The poet was given a seat near the king and the warrior was seated farther off. He was warned that if there was a marrow-bone on his dish he should not touch it, for there was a mighty warrior there whose privilege it was to take every marrow-bone. The stranger violated this custom, and then killed the mighty warrior. All rose up to avenge this outrage, but the stranger put them to flight, slaying many, and then sat down beside the poet. He told the king and queen they need have no fear. Then he took off his helmet, and his face was beautiful in the flush of battle.

The queen saw a ring on his finger that she had given twenty years before to her son, who had set out to learn feats of arms and never returned. The stranger said that he was her son, and she confirmed this by discovering under his right shoulder a grain of gold that she had placed there for luck and as a token of identity.[1] But the king would not believe it, for three other warriors had come in the past, claiming to be Conán, his only son. Next morning the true Conán, for this was he, set out and encountered each of the three pretenders. He slew the first two, who were impostors, but the third confessed that he was indeed a king's son, but not the son of Echaid, king of the Britons. He was the son of the king of Lochlann. His father had been killed treacherously by his own brother, and the prince, driven into exile, hoped to be accepted as Conán and so win the power to avenge his father. The two made peace and entered the fort. But the king required further proof. He had a fort on the border of the Britons' country at Dún Dá Lacha where there was a stone that a liar could not move, and there were two horses that a liar could not ride. Conán passed these tests and was acknowledged.

Then Congal assembled the hosts of the Saxons under their king Garb son of Rogarb,[2] and the hosts of France under their king Dairbre son of Dornmar, and of the Britons under Conán Rod and of Scotland under the four sons of Echaid the Yellow, Aed and Congal Mend and Suibne and Domnall Brecc. He led that great army to Ireland and gave battle to Domnall and the men of Ireland at Moira. And a great slaughter was made, and Congal fell there. 'These are the three virtues of the battle: the victory of Domnall in his truth over Congal in his falsehood, and that Suibne became a madman (on account of the number of poems he composed), and that one of the men of Scotland returned to his own country without ship or bark, with another warrior attached to him.'[3]

Cellach son of Mael Chaba, that is to say the son of Domnall's brother, slew Conán Rod in single combat. Of the Ulstermen only six hundred escaped; and of the foreigners one man alone, namely Dub Diad the druid, who flew through the air out of the battle and reached Scotland with a dead warrior attached to his leg. For Congal had tied his men in pairs so that one should not flee from another.

'That is the Feast of Dún na nGéd and the cause of the Battle of Moira.'

---

[1] Cf. 'The Birth of Brandub', cited p. 41.   [2] 'Fierce son of Very Fierce.'
[3] This version of the 'three virtues' recurs in a text quoted by O'Donovan, MR[2] 280, footnote. Cf. p. 56, note 2.

CATH MAIGE RÁTHA

THE BATTLE OF MOIRA

The story of the battle is preserved in two independent recensions. The first is Old Irish save for a few later forms, and may date from the early tenth century. It is preserved only in YBL (fcs. 209a48). The second is a long and tedious narrative of the worst period. From the style and language it cannot be earlier than *c.* 1300, and it may not be much earlier than the gathering of YBL (fcs. 299a1) that contains it (written in 1401).[1] Marstrander has made a comparative analysis of the three stories (*Ériu* 5, 228–9), but no attempt has yet been made to establish a relationship between them or to identify their sources.

The first recension of the Battle of Moira appears to be of historical value. The second recension has none. It is a late romance composed from earlier sources to which the author repeatedly refers without naming them. Some verse passages are borrowed from *Buile Shuibne*.[2] The first recension of the Battle of Moira (Marstrander's MR ii) is summarized here. It is noteworthy that it makes no mention of Suibne.

Ed. with translation, Marstrander, *Ériu* 5, 226–47. Numbers refer to lines of Marstrander's edition.

(1–34) The feast of Tara was held by Domnall son of Aed son of Ainmire. The three great feasts of Ireland were the feast of Emain, the feast of Tara, and the feast of Cruachain.

Domnall sat in the middle of the hall, with the king of Munster and his men on his right in the south end of the hall, the king of Connacht and his men in the west end of the hall behind him, the king of Ulster (*Ulaid*) and his men on the left in the north end of the hall, and the Leinstermen with their king to the east before him. (But when the kingship belonged to the Southern Uí Néill the king of Ailech sat on the left of the king of Ireland, and the king of Ulster further to the left.) (A poem follows in which a slightly different arrangement is prescribed, for here the kings of Munster and Leinster are on the right, and the kings of Ailech and Ulster on the left.)[3]

---

[1] s. Abbott and Gwynn, *Catalogue of Irish Manuscripts in Trinity College, Dublin, 344.* It is preserved also in four later MSS. (s. *Ériu* 5, 226), and was edited by O'Donovan for the Irish Archaeological Society (Dublin, 1842) from YBL, Stowe 23 K 44 and B iv 1. There is a fragment on a sixteenth-century leaf of LL (fcs. 409–10).

[2] s. O'Keeffe, *Buile Shuibne*[1] xxxiii.   [3] For a third tradition s. p. 61.

(35–60) Congal Caech king of Ulster, who was a fosterson of Domnall, sat therefore on the king's left hand. (He was called *caech* ('one-eyed') because once in king Domnall's orchard a bee had stung him in the eye. The Ulstermen had demanded the eye of the king's son in forfeit, but the matter was referred to Domnall for judgement and he had decreed only the destruction of the whole swarm so that the guilty bee should perish. The Ulstermen were not satisfied, and Congal had had a grievance ever since.) Food was served, and twelve eggs were brought to the couch of the king of Ireland. While Domnall stood to serve the eggs, Congal ate one of them. When the dishes were brought down there were only eleven eggs, and Domnall cursed the woman who had brought them for making a false count. 'I ate one of them,' said Congal. 'Finish them, then,' said Domnall, 'for I will not eat the remains of a theft.' 'You make a thief of me,' said Congal. 'I thank God, Domnall, that it is not after eating your food that I speak to you.' 'I shall give you an egg of gold,' said Domnall, 'and do not dispute with me about the egg.' Congal arose and called on his men to leave the feast, challenging Domnall to battle a month from that day.

(61–80) Congal went to Scotland to Domnall son of Echaid the Yellow, and returned a fortnight before the day of battle, bringing with him the men of Scotland. At first he quartered his men upon the Ulaid, but they complained. Then he went into Mag nGlass, the territory of Domnall's mother, and he left neither ox nor cow nor woman nor child there. Domnall assembled his army, and Congal set out to oppose him. The saints of Ireland sought to reconcile them, but Satan had entered into Congal and bade him not deny the word he had spoken before the men of Ireland. He should not prosper if he denied it, but if he were victorious he would be king of Ireland.

(81–129) Domnall pitched his tent and was playing chess with one of his men, while a dwarf sat on the ridge-pole on guard. For dwarfs have keen eyes and sharp wits. Dúnchad, a chosen warrior and faithful friend of Domnall, was entrusted with the battle against Congal, with his two foster-brothers to aid him.

The battle lasted three full days, one province making the attack against Congal each day.[1] There was a great slaughter,

---

[1] Apparently Munster, Leinster, and Connacht. But later the armies of

and the clamour of battle was loud and blood was freely shed. Mighty was the thunder of clashing shields and smiting swords and rattling quivers, and so forth. Though a raven should light upon Congal's eye, he dared not brush it off, on account of the skill and speed and ferocity of Dúnchad. Dúnchad killed Congal's horse, and he gave him his own horse. He split Congal's shield, and he gave him his own shield. He broke his sword and gave him his own sword. Whenever Congal advanced the battle gathered against him. 'Who makes this charge?' said Congal. 'The Leinstermen,' they said. 'We fear them not,' said he. 'It is the valour of hounds on a dunghill.' Thus he derided in turn the men of Munster, Connacht, Ossory, and the Southern Uí Néill. But when he heard that the Northern Uí Néill were come against him, he said that he feared that mass of shields, for one could go neither through it nor past it. 'How is Domnall now?' he asked. And when he heard that Domnall was praying to God, he said that he would go to submit to him.

(129–56) Congal went around the battlefield to the king's tent. 'Halt, Congal!' said the warriors. 'I go to submit to Domnall,' said he, 'so that the men of Ireland may see me submit to him, as they have seen me rise against him.' 'Wait a while, Congal,' said Domnall. 'We have sent two hostages to the house of the King of Truth so that he may give us judgement in our dispute and we may accept it.' 'It shall not be so!' said Congal. 'It shall be so!' said Domnall.

Then Congal met Conall Clocach, the king's jester, in the battle, and asked him to sing a quatrain showing who would be victorious. (The jester's quatrain is obscure. Congal says it is false and repeats it in an emended form, also obscure to me.) 'It is true,' said Congal. 'I shall be killed there.' Then he attacked like a mad bull, and rushed through the battle until he came against Dúnchad and cut off his head. The watchman said that he did not like the music of the battle.

(157–67) Then Domnall himself went into the fight, calling on the name of God; and when the men of Ireland saw Domnall's face, they made a charge so mighty that they overwhelmed the Ulstermen, and Congal Cendfoda was slain. Then there was so great a slaughter that not one of the men of Scotland escaped,

Leinster, Munster, Connacht, Ossory, Southern Uí Néill and Northern Uí Néill are mentioned as taking part.

save one man only; and he escaped by swimming. 'What news?' said Domnall son of Echaid. 'Give me a drink,' said the warrior. They gave him a cup of ale and he drank it at one draught. 'Give me another drink,' said he. They gave him another cup and he drank it; and so he drank three cups of ale. 'What news?' said Domnall. 'What news do you ask?' said he. 'You shall never see a man of those who went from here, save me alone.' Then he died.

(168–245) The heads were brought to Domnall son of Aed, and among them the heads of Dúnchad and his foster-brothers. Domnall lamented the three warriors in a quatrain, and he lamented Faelchu, king of Meath, his mother's son, who had fallen in the battle too. Then Congal was borne into his abandoned enclosure, and the corpse was washed, and his head was placed on the rampart of the fort. Domnall then lamented his fallen enemy. (This lament, in 46 lines of verse, brings the tale to an end.)

BUILE SHUIBNE

THE FRENZY OF SUIBNE

The text is preserved in two paper manuscripts (B and K) in the Royal Irish Academy's collection, and there is a summary recension in one of the O'Clery manuscripts (Brussels 3410, 59a–61b) written in 1629. This summary (L) is the earliest of the three manuscripts, and refers to 'the book named *Buile Shuibne*', but it seems to derive from a late copy independent of the exemplar of B; and K represents a third tradition. The text belongs to the twelfth century in its present form, but it proclaims itself a compilation from earlier sources; and there is a well-known poem attributed to Suibne the Madman in a ninth-century manuscript of Priscian (*Thes. Pal.* ii 294), so the tradition is old. The Old Norse *Speculum Regale*, a thirteenth-century document, mentions as one of the wonders of Ireland the wild men of the woods who lose their wits in the din of battle (*Ériu* 4, 11. § 18). The story is distinguished for the verse passages which make up the greater part of the text, some of them being nature poetry of considerable merit. Grosjean suggests that the prose narrative is a mere framework used by an editor who wished to make a collection of poems about Suibne (s. *Anal. Boll.* 50, 444).

Ed. with translation, O'Keeffe from B, with variants from K, and the summary L in an appendix, ITS xii (1913); reprinted without translation, Med. and Mod. Irish Series i (1931).

(1–6) Suibne son of Colmán was king of Dál nAraide.[1] One day Saint Rónán was marking the boundaries of a church in that county, and Suibne heard the sound of his bell. When his people told him that Rónán was establishing a church in his territory, he set out in anger to expel the cleric. His wife Eorann sought to restrain him, and caught the border of his cloak, but he rushed naked from the house, leaving the cloak in her hands. Rónán was chanting the Office when Suibne came up, and the king seized the psalter and threw it into the lake. He then laid hands on the saint and was dragging him away, when a messenger arrived from Congal Claen to summon him to the battle of Moira. Suibne departed with the messenger leaving Rónán sorrowful. Next day an otter from the lake restored the psalter to the saint unharmed. Rónán gave thanks to God and cursed the king, wishing that he might wander naked through the world as he had come naked into his presence.

(7–10) Rónán went to Moira to make peace between Domnall and Congal Claen, but without success. He and his clerics sprinkled holy water on the armies, but when they sprinkled it on Suibne he slew one of the clerics with a spear and made a second cast at Rónán himself. The second spear broke against the saint's bell, and the shaft flew into the air. Rónán cursed Suibne, wishing that he might fly through the air like the shaft of his spear, and that he might die of a spear-cast like the cleric whom he had slain.

(11–15) Thereafter, when the battle was joined, the armies on both sides raised three mighty shouts. Suibne was terrified by the clamour. His weapons fell from his hands. He was seized with trembling and fled in a frenzy like a bird of the air. His feet rarely touched the ground in his flight, and at last he settled upon a yew-tree far from the battlefield. There he was discovered by a kinsman, Aongus the Fat, who had fled the field after the victory of Domnall. Aongus sought to persuade Suibne to join him, but Suibne flew away like a bird and came to Tír Conaill where he perched on a tree near the church called Cell Riagáin. It happened that the victorious army of Domnall had encamped there after the battle. Domnall recognized him and lamented his misfortune.

[1] A territory south of Dál Riada, bordering on Loch Neagh. It included parts of south County Antrim and of County Down.

(16) (In a short poem Domnall reproaches Suibne for his part in the battle. Part of the poem, however, is a dialogue between Domnall and Congal and is out of place here.)

(17) Suibne fled again and was for a long time travelling through Ireland till he came to Glenn Bolcáin.

> 'It was there that the madmen used to abide when their year of frenzy was over, for that valley is always a place of great delight to madmen. Glenn Bolcáin has four gaps to the wind and a lovely fragrant wood and clean-bordered wells and cool springs, and a sandy stream of clear water with green cress and long waving brooklime on its surface.'

(26-7) For seven years Suibne wandered throughout Ireland, and then he returned to Glenn Bolcáin. There Loingsechán came to seek him. (Some say that Loingsechán was a son of Suibne's mother, some say that he was his foster-brother, but, however that may be, he was a faithful friend, for he rescued Suibne three times.[1]) Loingsechán found the footprints of Suibne near the river where he used to come to eat watercress, and the trace of his passage from tree to tree in the broken branches, but he found not Suibne. He slept one night in a hut, and Suibne came near and heard him snore. And he uttered a lay:

> 'The man by the wall snores: I dare not sleep like that. For seven years since that Tuesday at Moira I have not slept for a moment.
>
> .   .   .   .
>
> 'The cress of the well of Druim Cirb is my meal at terce. My face betrays it. Truly I am Suibne the Madman.
>
> .   .   .   .
>
> 'Though I live from hill to hill on the mountain above the valley of yews, alas! that I was not left to lie with Congal Claen.
>
> .   .   .   .
>
> 'Green cress and a drink of clear water is my fare. I do not smile. This is not the fate of the man by the wall.'
>
> .   .   .   .

---

[1] The text records only two occasions below. This first attempt fails, but it is included in the reckoning.

(31–3) Eorann, Suibne's wife, had gone to live with Guaire, one of the claimants to the kingdom. Suibne visited her and spoke of their former happiness together, of her present comfort and his misery. Their dialogue is in verse. He reproaches her for enjoying the love of another man and the comfort of his house while her husband is an outcast, and she protests that she would rather live with Suibne in the wilderness than with any man of Ireland or Scotland. Suibne tells her that she does better to stay with Guaire than to share the life of a madman, and that he bears her no grudge. As people approach he flies away.

(35) Suibne came to Ros Ercáin where he had had a house, and he settled in a yew tree there. Loingsechán came again to capture him. At first he pleaded with him to return home and resume the royal comforts that had been his. Suibne bade Loingsechán leave him to his fate, and asked for news of his country.

'"Your father is dead." "That grieves me," said he. "Your mother is dead," said the lad. "Now all pity for me is at an end," said he. "Your brother is dead," said Loing-sechán. "I am sorely wounded by that," said Suibne. "Your daughter is dead," said Loingsechán. "And an only daughter is the needle of the heart," said Suibne. "Dead is your son who used to call you 'Father'," said Loingsechán. "Indeed," said he, "that is the drop that brings a man to the ground."'

(36–40) (This dialogue is repeated in verse in a greatly expanded form.) When Suibne heard of the death of his son he fell down from the tree, and Loingsechán seized and bound him, and then told him that all his kindred were alive. Soon he recovered his reason and was king again, but he remained in the custody of Loingsechán. One day an old woman reminded him of his frenzy, and so excited him that he flew away, and the hag followed him ; and when at length he alighted on a tree she perched on a tree beside him. Then Suibne heard the cry of hunters and the bellowing of the stag, and he made a poem in praise of the trees of Ireland and in memory of his hardships:

'O lowing stag, sweet clamourer, dear to me is the music thou makest in the valley.'

Oak, alder, black-thorn, apple-tree, briar, yew, holly, birch and aspen are addressed in turn, and then he remembers his happy life as king and laments his fate. Then nature is praised in the spirit of some of the Fenian ballads:

'The starry frost will come, falling on every pool. I am wretched, wandering exposed to it on the mountain.

'The herons call in cold Glenn Aigle, swift flocks of birds coming and going.

'I love not the prattle that men and women make: sweeter to me is the song of the blackbird on his perch.

'I love not the trumpeting I hear in the morning: sweeter to me is the squeal of the badger in Benna Broc.

'I love not the loud horn I hear: sweeter to me is the belling of a twenty-pointed stag.

.   .   .   .

'The curse of fair-haired Rónán has made me thy companion, lowing stag, sweet clamourer.'

(This poem of sixty-five quatrains is in a bold metre, lines of seven syllables ending in a trisyllabic word alternating with lines of five syllables ending in a monosyllable, and the metre is well handled. It is followed by two others of similar temper, one of twenty-three quatrains, the other of thirty-two, each in a different metre.)

(55–61) After other adventures, Suibne went again to visit his wife, but refused to enter the house for fear that his people would confine him there. Eorann said that, since he would not stay with her, he had best be gone and not return, for she was ashamed that people should see him in his madness. In a short poem Suibne laments the frailty of women and recalls his feats of battle when he was king. Then he flies away to Benn Boirche. (Two poems follow, the first somewhat in the spirit of Marbán's account of his life as a hermit,[1] the second another lament for his misery.)

(63–5) Then his reason returned to Suibne and he sought to return to his people; but that was revealed to Saint Rónán, and he prayed that Suibne might not be allowed to return to persecute the Church as he had done before. When the madman was on his way, he was beset by a fearful apparition of headless

[1] s. Kuno Meyer, *Ancient Irish Poetry* 47.

bodies and trunkless heads which pursued him through the air with frightful clamour until he escaped from them into the clouds.

(74–83) At last Suibne came to the monastery of Saint Mo Ling. (In a poem of fifteen quatrains in dialogue between the saint and the madman, Suibne foretells his death by the hand of a herdsman.) Mo Ling made him welcome, and bade him return from his wanderings every evening so that his history might be written. For it was destined that his story should be written there and that he should receive a Christian burial. Mo Ling bade his cook give supper to Suibne, and, wherever he travelled during the day, he would return at night. The cook would thrust her foot into some cowdung and fill the hole with milk, and Suibne would lie down to drink. But the cook's husband, who was a herd, grew jealous of this attention by his wife, and he slew Suibne with a spear as he lay drinking the milk one evening. (Others say that the herd placed the point of a deer's horn on the spot where Suibne used to drink, and that he fell upon it and so died.) Before his death he confessed his sin and received the body of Christ and was anointed. (The conversation of Suibne, Mo Ling and Mongán the herdsman is recorded in a poem of twenty-six quatrains. Suibne says:)

'Sweeter to me once than the sound of a bell beside me was the song of a blackbird on the mountain and the belling of the stag in a storm.

'Sweeter to me once than the voice of a lovely woman beside me was the voice of the mountain grouse at dawn.

'Sweeter to me once was the cry of wolves than the voice of a cleric within, bleating and whining.

'Though you like to drink your ale in taverns with honour, I would rather drink water from my hand taken from the well in theft.

'Though sweet to you yonder in the church the smooth words of your students, sweeter to me the noble chant of the hounds of Glenn Bolcáin.'

.   .   .   .

(84–5) Then Suibne swooned, and Mo Ling and his clerics brought each a stone for his monument, and Mo Ling said:

'Here is the tomb of Suibne. His memory grieves my

heart. Dear to me for love of him is every place the holy madman frequented.

.   .   .   .

'Dear to me each cool stream on which the green cress grew, dear each well of clear water, for Suibne used to visit them.

'If the King of the stars allows it, arise and go with me. Give me, O heart, thy hand, and come from the tomb.

'Sweet to me was the conversation of Suibne: long shall I remember it. I pray to the chaste King of Heaven over his grave and tomb.'

(86) Suibne rose out of his swoon, and Mo Ling took him by the hand, and they went together to the door of the church. And Suibne leaned against the doorpost and gave a great sigh, and his spirit went to Heaven, and he was buried with honour by Mo Ling.

(87) Thus far some of the tales and adventures of Suibne son of Colmán Cuar, king of Dál nAraide. *Finis.*

THE CYCLE OF DIARMAIT SON OF AED SLÁINE
AND GUAIRE AIDNE, A.D. 643

DIARMAIT and Bláthmac[1] sons of Aed Sláine became joint kings of Ireland in 642 and died in 664. Guaire Aidne, famous for his hospitality, was king of Connacht and died in 662 (AU *s.a.* 662). Diarmait and Guaire appear as enemies in 'The Battle of Carn Conaill' (*Cath Cairn Chonaill*),[2] Diarmait overcoming Guaire and then yielding to him on account of his great charity. One other tale about Diarmait has come down to us and is presented here. Guaire is the central figure of the important group of stories that follows it.

TOCHMARC BECFOLA
THE WOOING OF BECFOLA

The story is extant in two recensions, one of which is early, the other a late Middle Irish or early Modern Irish redaction. The former is preserved in a gathering of YBL written in 1391 (fcs. 117b43–119a35) and in H.3.18 (p. 756, 16th century). The latter is in BM Eg. 1781 (150b, 15th century); it is a poor performance, lacking important parts of the story. The relationship of Eg. to Y and H is not clear to me, and may prove hard to establish. A new edition of the early recension is desirable. The neuter gender is well preserved, the independent pronoun does not occur, and some early verbal forms have been retained. The common source of Y and H was written in the Old Irish period, not later than the ninth century. The early recension is summarized here.

Ed. with translation, O'Looney, RIA MSS. Ser. I i 172 (Y with variant readings from H); O'Grady SG i 85 = ii 91 (Eg.).[3]

Diarmait son of Aed Sláine was king of Tara, and Crimthann son of Aed was in fosterage with him as a hostage from Leinster. They went one day to Áth Truim,[4] and met a woman coming eastward across the ford in a chariot. She wore a gold-

---

[1] The correct form is *Blaimac* or *Blámac* according to Paul Walsh, IHS 2, 445.

[2] Ed. Stokes, ZCP 3, 203–19, cf. Fragmentary Annals, SG i 396–400 = ii 431–6.

[3] James Stephens tells the story in his *Irish Fairy Tales*, p. 133.

[4] 'The Ford of Trom', i.e. Trim, Co. Meath.

embroidered smock, and a crimson cloak held by a brooch of gold set with precious stones. A golden diadem was on her head, and her collar and shoes were of gold. The chariot was drawn by two dark grey horses with gold bridles, and their yokes were decorated with silver ornaments.

Diarmait asked whence she came and whither she was going, and she replied that she came from no great distance and was in search of seed wheat. 'If you will have the seed of this country,' said Diarmait, 'I alone have what is worthy of you.' 'I shall not refuse,' said she, 'if the bride-price is paid.' 'You shall have this little pin,' said Diarmait. 'I will accept it,' said she. He takes her to Tara, but cannot tell her name. When the people ask what bride-price he has paid, he tells them that he gave his little pin. 'It is small wealth,' say all. The druid says: 'Becfola ("Small Wealth") will be her name.'

Becfola desired the love of Crimthand and he gave her a tryst at the hour of terce on Sunday at Cluain Dá Chaillech, but his people forbade him to abduct the wife of the High King. She set out, however, with her maid on the pretence that she had left certain possessions at Cluain Dá Chaillech, and wished to recover them. The king protested against this violation of Sunday,[1] but Becfola persisted.

On their way southward from Tara, the women went astray, and as night fell they were attacked by wolves who devoured the maid. Becfola took refuge in a tree. She saw a fire in the forest and went towards it. A warrior was cooking a pig over the fire. He was clad in a silk shirt embroidered with circles of gold and silver. A helmet of gold, silver and crystal was on his head; and so forth. Becfola sat by the fire. The warrior looked at her, but paid her no further heed. When he had finished his cooking, he washed his hands and went away. She followed him to a lake. There was a boat of bronze in the lake attached by a cable to the shore and by another cable to an island. The

---

[1] A reference to *Cáin Domnaig* ('The Law of Sunday'), a part of which, belonging to the ninth century, was edited by O'Keeffe, *Ériu* 2, 189–214. The prohibition of travel is mentioned in § 23, p. 204. This text is an Irish version of the Epistle of Jesus concerning Sunday, s. Priebsch, MLR 2, 138 (1907). The Old Irish law-tract on the observance of Sunday, which is the *Cáin Domnaig* proper, is printed Anec. iii 21–7, and the prohibition of travel appears on p. 21. An English translation by Donald Maclean has been published: *The Law of the Lord's Day in the Celtic Church* (Edinburgh, Clark, 1926).

warrior hauled in the boat and Becfola got into it. They went to the island and she went before him into a house. They ate and drank, but did not speak. He lay down and she lay beside him, but he did not turn towards her throughout the night.

In the morning they heard a cry, summoning Fland to battle. The warrior took up his weapons and went out. Becfola watched from the door and saw three others on the shore of the island like unto the warrior in form and age and beauty. She saw four others along by the island with their shields on guard. The warrior and his three companions fought against the other four till all were wounded. They separated, and the warrior returned alone.

Becfola praised the warrior's valour, but he said only that it were well if it had been against enemies. These were the sons of his father's brother, and his companions were his own three brothers. He was Fland grandson of Fedach, and the grandsons of Fedach were fighting for the Island of Fedach Mac In Daill.[1] Becfola offered to stay with him, but he replied that it would be a poor marriage for her to leave the king of Ireland and share the life of a wandering soldier. 'Why should we not be lovers now?' said she. 'Not now,' said he; 'but if the island be mine, and if we live, I shall come to fetch you, and you shall be my wife always. And now go!' She regrets the maid, and he tells her that the girl is alive at the foot of the tree. The warriors of the island are with her and will accompany them home.

Becfola reached home to find Diarmait rising on the same Sunday morning. He was glad that she had not travelled on a Sunday, and she said that she did not dare to disobey him, as though she had not gone at all. But from that time she used to say:

'I spent a night in the forest, in the house on the Island of Mac In Daill. Though I was with a man, it was no sin: it was none too soon when we parted.

'The island of Fedach Mac In Daill in Dubthar in Leinster, although it is close to the road, bearded youths do not find it.'

Everyone used to wonder at this.

A year from that day Fland came badly wounded to the door. Becfola greeted him with a quatrain and he replied with a

---

[1] 'son of the blind man.'

quatrain. She went from the house and followed him, and could not be found. Diarmait told his people to let her go unhindered, for it was not known who was going nor who had come.

As they were speaking, four young clerics came into the house. Diarmait covered his face in horror at the sight of clerics travelling on a Sunday. But they explained that their journey was no mere wantonness, but that Saint Mo Laise of Devinish[1] had sent them. That morning there had been a great fight on the island between two parties of four warriors each, from which only one man had come alive, and he was badly wounded. Mo Laise had buried the seven dead, and from their clothes and ornaments and weapons there was taken as much gold and silver as two men could carry. The clerics had come to ask how much of the treasure trove the king would claim as his share. Diarmait said that he would take no share of what God had sent to the saint.

'That is the silver and gold with which the sacred emblems of Mo Laise were decorated, namely his shrine and his satchel and his crozier. But Becfola went with Fland grandson of Fedach, and she has not since returned. That is The Wooing of Becfola. Finit.'

Guaire is the subject of various anecdotes, one of which appears in Kuno Meyer's *King and Hermit*.[2] Two others, known also from independent sources,[3] are included in the entry on Guaire in the Fragmentary Annals edited from Eg. 1782 (f. 57) in O'Grady's *Silva Gadelica* i 396–401 = ii 431–7. Indeed the so-called Annals consist at this point of a summary of the Battle of Carn Conaill and the two anecdotes in question. There are three longer tales which deserve notice here. The first is of special interest as it presents an Irish parallel to the story of Tristan and Isolde, itself known to be of Irish origin, so that we have here a precious document. In the second Guaire appears as a jealous, crafty and cruel man, in contradiction of the common tradition regarding him, so that the composition seems to reflect the bias of an enemy of Connacht. The third story deals with the arrogance of the poets, an abuse which had been the subject of legislation at the Assembly of Druim Cett in 575, and

---

[1] Devinish Island in Loch Erne.
[2] s. Meyer, *Ancient Irish Poetry* 47.
[3] s. Abbott and Gwynn, *Catalogue* 105, 347. The Guaire anecdotes here (YBL fcs. 133a1) follow the Battle of Carn Conaill. Keating's account (iii 59–71) seems to derive in part from the Fragmentary Annals.

also with the discovery of the Táin, which is credited to the famous poet Senchán Torpeist. Thurneysen has suggested that this tradition that Senchán was the first to compose a written narrative may be genuine, since the existence of a written tradition going back to the sixth century is now established (ZCP 19, 209).

SCÉLA CANO MEIC GARTNÁIN
THE STORY OF CANO SON OF GARTNÁN

The story is preserved only in YBL (fcs. 128a46), and has been assigned by Thurneysen to a date *c.* 900. He has shown that it is a romance of no historical value, since the chronology is impossible. Cano died in 688 and cannot therefore have come to Ireland bearing arms in the lifetime of Aedán Mac Gabráin (†606). Moreover the expedition from Scotland to Ireland is recorded in the Annals of Ulster *s.a.* 667, when Diarmait and Guaire were already dead, so that Cano could not have taken part in Diarmait's campaign against Guaire. Finally these two kings were not contemporaries of Aedán Mac Gabráin. The story is thus an example of historical romance, in which historical events and persons are woven into a single narrative without regard for chronology.[1] It is important as a picture of the manners of its time, and especially for the Tristan-motif that forms a part of it.[2] The parallel rests upon the love-theme, the fact that Créd is the young wife of an old king whose name is Marcán (diminutive of Marc), and the final episode in which Cano approaches the coast of Ireland in a ship, Créd dies before he reaches land, and he dies soon afterwards. The motif of the love-potion does not occur.

Joseph Loth amplified Thurneysen's discussion, and while stressing the absence of an important feature of the Tristan story, inasmuch as Cano is not akin to Marcán, he recognized its importance, seeing the essential parallel in the motif of heroic fidelity in love, sealed at last by death.[3] He supposed, however, that Cano is bound in honour by the obligation of hospitality, and pointed out that the conflict between passion and duty, the moral drama which dominates the story of Tristan and Isolde, is a Celtic motif, as was shown by him, RC 30, 270. Gaston Paris had seen there a German influence, while Bédier considered it a French creation. Loth regards the story of Cano as a further Irish example, but we shall see that this interpretation rests upon a misunderstanding.

[1] So, according to Bédier, the *Chansons de geste* are learned compositions written in the eleventh century, in which the fictions that had grown up around the memory of Charlemagne and other heroes are woven together (s. Nitze, *Modern Philology* 39, 2).

[2] s. Thurneysen, ZRP 43, 385–8. He points out that the love-potion is absent here. [3] *Comptes rendus de l'Acad.* 1923, 122–33.

It remains to be said that there are some points of contact between this story and 'The Wooing of Becfola'. There Crimthand, the fosterson of Diarmait, and the mysterious Fland are the lovers of Becfola; here Colcu, son of Marcán and stepson of Créd, and the stranger Cano; although Colcu is here rejected by Créd.[1] The refusal by Fland of Becfola's first approach has a close parallel in Cano's refusal of Cred, and suggests a different interpretation from that put forward by Loth. Fland will not marry Becfola while he is in exile as a mercenary soldier, because that would be for her a poor exchange for the life of a queen. Cano's refusal is apparently for the same reason, not on account of any obligation to the king. But the obligation of honour is the motive in the case of Crimthand and also in the case of Mael Fothartaig (p. 42). It might be considered whether these stories have borrowed a motif from the story of Joseph, *Genesis* xxxix; but I do not dispute the Celtic origin of the conflict between passion and duty, so far as the medieval romances are concerned.

Ed. Meyer, Anec. i 1–15; translation, Thurneysen, ZRP 43, 388–402. The numbers indicate the paragraphs of Thurneysen's translation.

(1–4) Aedán son of Gabrán and Gartnán, his own son, were rivals for the kingdom of Scotland, so that half the men of Scotland fell in battle. Gartnán lived in the island of Skye in great splendour and comfort. A son was born to him, namely Cano son of Gartnán, and he sent the child away in fosterage. One winter's night Aedán attacked the island with two thousand men, and Gartnán and his people perished. Cano resolved to flee to Ireland, and ordered boats to be built. With fifty warriors and their wives and fifty servants he sailed to Ireland.

(5–10) At that time Diarmait and Bláthmac sons of Aed Sláine were in Ulster enjoying their royal privilege of hospitality, and they received Cano with honour. But Aedán sent messengers with a great treasure of gold and silver that he had seized in Skye, offering it to the kings if they would kill Cano. Diarmait's daughter was in love with Cano on account of his fame, before she had seen him. She overheard the message of the Scots and warned Cano. Her warning is spoken in five quatrains, of which the meaning is veiled, but Cano understands. He went before the kings, and Diarmait told him that they would not sell his life though the whole house should be

---

[1] The stepson motif recurs in the story of Mael Fothartaig (p. 42).

filled with treasure. Bláthmac followed him out and advised him
to pursue the messengers, and attack them as soon as they left
the territory and were no longer under the king's protection, and
so to recover his father's treasure. Cano took them by surprise
at sea, but let them go unharmed, and Diarmait praised him;
for it had been revealed to Diarmait that Cano's restraint would
be rewarded. He would be king of Scotland after Aedán for
twenty-four years.

(11) Cano went across the Shannon into Connacht to visit
Guaire, and came to the house of Marcán[1] whose wife was Créd
daughter of Guaire. She had loved Cano before he came to
Ireland. Moreover he had protected her home when he came
with Diarmait to give battle to Guaire.[2] Cano sought the protection of Créd on his journey to the court of Guaire. Colcu son
of Marcán intervened (the text is obscure here), and was re-
pulsed by Créd who declared her love for Cano.

(12–15) Cano arrived at the court of Guaire at Derlus and was
made welcome. He stayed for three months, and one-third of
the dwelling was occupied by Guaire, one-third by Cano and
one-third by Senchán, *fili* to Guaire and all the men of Ireland.
(Here there is a digression into anecdotes about Senchán.)
Senchán protested against the expense of so much hospitality.
He and Guaire were a sufficient burden upon the Connachtmen.
He contrived by magic to scatter Cano's men when they were
out hunting so that they could not find each other. They took
leave of Guaire and announced that they were going into
Munster to visit Illann son of Scannlán. Guaire bade them to a
last feast and summoned the nobles of Connacht to take leave
of them. Créd and Marcán and Colcu came to the feast, and
Créd asked Guaire to be allowed to pour out the wine for the
men of Scotland and of Connacht that night. She put a sleep-
charm upon all the company save herself and Cano.[3] She went
to him and entreated him, but he would not be her lover so long

---

[1] Marcán is king of Hy Many in the story of Cellach (p. 87).

[2] This refers to the Battle of Carn Conaill, fought in 649, but there is no
mention of the episode until now, and Cano does not figure in the versions of
that story that have come down to us. It was in this battle that Dinertach
was slain, and there is a beautiful lament for his death, attributed to Cred
daughter of Guaire, s. *Ériu* i, 15, and Meyer, *Ancient Irish Poetry* 63.

[3] So did Gráinne in 'The Pursuit of Diarmaid and Gráinne' (ed. O'Grady,
Trans. Oss. Soc. vi) p. 53.

as he was a mercenary soldier. If he should become king he
would come to fetch her and she would be his wife always.[1]
He gave her a stone as a pledge that they would meet again.
He said that his life was in the stone. When his mother was
in childbed, she had seen in a dream two fairy women approach
her. Then his life had come out of her mouth in the form of a
stone, and she snatched it from the hand of one of the women.
The woman said: 'It is the life of your son that you hold.'
His mother had kept the stone till he was able to protect it.

(16) Cano went to Illann son of Scannlán and was made
welcome. Illann promised that though he had been sold for
silver by the sons of Aed, and left hungry by Guaire,[2] he should
lack nothing in Corco Laige. He asked the assurance of his
people and of his wife that they would provide hospitality. His
people promised three oxen, three salted pigs, and three vats
of ale every evening, in addition to their regular tribute. His
wife promised three herds of seven-score cows. Then Illann
ventured to join his guests and promised that Cano and his
followers would be welcome to stay with him until Cano became
king of Scotland. They stayed for three years without seeking
entertainment elsewhere for a single night. A hundred and fifty
loads of wood were brought in each morning and evening, and
Illann feared that his forests would be destroyed. Cano said
that before the forests perished Illann himself would perish.

(17) Then hostages from Scotland came to guarantee the
kingdom to Cano (presumably announcing the death of Aedán).
For two days there was general lamentation for Cano's departure, and then he set out. Illann foretold his own death within
a year, and bestowed upon Cano fifty dark-grey horses, fifty
copper cauldrons, and fifty harnesses.

(18) A year from that day Illann was slain and his dwelling
plundered by men of his own kindred. Cano was fishing from
a boat upon the sea, and a wave of blood came into his boat.
He stood up and clapped his hands in mourning. (His lamentation is given in a poem of fourteen quatrains.)

(19–20) Then the Saxons, Britons and Scots went with Cano
to Corco Laige, and he slew the slayers of Illann and restored

---

[1] So Fland in 'The Wooing of Becfola' (p. 77).
[2] This hardly implies an alternative tradition, but may be a part of Illann's
boasting.

his dwelling and established his son as king, and took hostages for the new king's safety. Thereafter Cano was in Scotland as king, and he remembered the hospitality of Illann.

(21) He used to make a yearly tryst with Créd at Inber Colptha.[1] Colcu son of Marcán was there each time with a hundred warriors. At last they made a tryst at Loch Créda in the north. She went northward bringing the stone with her. He came from the east so that they were already within sight of each other. Colcu[2] came with three ships and wounded him, so that he escaped from the ship with difficulty. When Créd saw his face (covered with blood?), she shattered her head against a rock, and the stone broke as she fell. Cano died three days after he had gone east (to Scotland).[3]

'This is the story of Cano son of Gartnán and Créd daughter of Guaire.'

CAITHRÉIM CELLAIG
THE NOBLE CAREER OF CELLACH

The story is preserved in two recensions, one earlier than the other. The older recension is represented by the Lebor Brecc (fcs. 272b11, early fifteenth century), and a copy of that manuscript made by Michael O'Clery in 1629 (Brussels 2324–40). The language points to a date c. 1200.[4] The later recension is represented by the Liber Flavus Fergusiorum (c. 1440) and YBL (Nat. Lib. Philipps Collection 8214, col. 982, not included in the published facsimile), and has been assigned to the fourteenth century by K. Mulchrone. Like the preceding story this is romance, not history, for Cellach must have flourished in the sixth century,[5] and cannot have been a contemporary of Guaire; but the tradition that Cellach was murdered at the instigation of Guaire is recorded in the Dindshenchas, RC 16, 139 = Metr. Dinds. iii 414, cf. Hy Fiachra p. 32. Domnall and Fergus became joint kings of Ireland in 565, and St. Ciarán died in 549, so that there is no anachronism so far as they are concerned. There is some reason to believe that the story was composed around the poems it contains, for they are directly quoted in the prose.[6] Two

---

[1] The mouth of the River Boyne.
[2] Lit. 'He comes', but Colcu is evidently meant.
[3] His death is recorded in the Annals of Tigernach, RC 17, 210 = FM 686.
[4] The infixed pronoun is rare, and the verbal inflexion is late Middle Irish.
[5] His father Éogan Bél died in 542 (AU).
[6] s. Grosjean, Anal. Boll. 52, p. 422; Mulchrone, Caithréim Cellaig, xi. Grosjean thinks that the authors of prose and verse are different persons;

of these poems constitute the chief literary merit of the text. They are well known from Sigerson's translations in his *Bards of the Gael and Gall*. The earlier recension is summarized here. The corresponding lines of Dr. Mulchrone's edition are supplied.

Ed. with translation, O'Grady, SG i 49–65 = ii 50–69 (LB); ed. Kathleen Mulchrone, *Caithréim Cellaig*, Med. and Mod. Ir. Ser. iv, 1933 (Y with readings from the *Liber Flavus*).

(1–73) Eogan Bél king of Connacht took the spoils of every province in turn. The men of Munster and Leinster submitted to him and did him service. But there was fierce conflict between Connacht and Ulster, although Ulster was commonly worsted in the struggle, all three territories of Clanna Néill, namely Conall, Eogan and Oriel. There were two kings in Ulster at that time, Fergus and Domnall, the kings of Conall and Eogan respectively, and they led a great hosting against Connacht, and were at first successful in plundering Connacht as far as the River Moy. But Eogan Bél routed them at the battle of Sligo, though he came with only one battalion against five battalions from Ulster. Domnall and Fergus were killed in the battle, and Eogan Bél was so badly wounded that he was borne on a litter from the field.

(74–134) As he lay dying Eogan advised his people to make his son Cellach king in his stead, since Muiredach, the younger son, was not yet of age. Cellach was a monk of Clonmacnoise, and Eogan bade the men of Hy Fiachrach ask St. Ciarán to release him from his vows. He then gave instructions for his own burial, that he should be buried on the border of his territory, spear in hand, facing northward against Ulster, and foretold that so long as his face was turned towards them, the men of Ulster would not prevail against Connacht. (But the men of Ulster later removed his body and buried him face downwards near Loch Gill.) The men of Hy Fiachrach went to Clonmacnoise and made their petition to St. Ciarán, and he refused to grant it. But they persuaded Cellach to come away with them without the permission of his abbot. St. Ciarán cursed Cellach for this violation of his vow of obedience and prayed that he might die a violent death.

Cellach became king of northern Hy Fiachrach, and Guaire was

Dr. Mulchrone suggests that the poet later added the prose narrative to his verse composition.

king of Hy Fiachrach of Aidne at the time, and at the height of his power. There was rivalry between them and a dispute about their respective territories; and Guaire invited Cellach to a meeting and attacked him by treachery, so that most of his followers were killed, and he escaped with difficulty.

(135–98) For a year Cellach was in the wilderness, and he was seized with repentance for his disobedience and remorse on account of the curse that he had drawn down upon himself. And he spoke this lay:

'Unhappy he who leaves the cloister for any worldly life, who leaves the great love of God to be a king in the world of mortal men. Unhappy he who takes up arms in this world, unless he do penance. Better are white books for recitation of the Office.

'Though the art of war is a worthy art, it is a great labour for a little gain: it is a meagre life that comes of it, and hell is its reward.

'The art of the robber is a wicked art, a wandering needy life of thievery: though he be a good man who chooses it, it makes him evil.

'All of these wrongs are done by Cellach son of Eogan, as he wanders throughout Cera[1] from end to end, pursued by wicked men.

'Unhappy he who abandons holy heaven where the saints abide for the gloomy hell of the damned, who abandons the great Lord, O Christ, thou Lord of battles!'

Then Cellach returned to Clonmacnoise, and was pardoned by St. Ciarán; and his followers chose Muiredach as their king and were faithful to him.

(199–256) The Holy Spirit had come into the soul of Cellach, and he advanced in learning and sanctity, so that the clergy of his country elected him bishop of Killala. And on one occasion he came on visitation into the neighbourhood of Durlas where Guaire dwelt. The king summoned him into his presence, but it was noon on a Saturday when the messengers arrived, and Cellach replied that he would not violate the Sabbath. Either the king might come to hear mass on Sunday and meet him afterwards, or he would go to wait upon the king on

---

[1] The barony of Carra, County Mayo, s. Hog. Onom.

Monday. Guaire was angry and sent a message ordering Cellach to quit the country that same night, or the church would be burnt over his head. Cellach disregarded this order and remained where he was till Monday.

(256–669) Cellach retired as a hermit on to an island in a lake, and there remained with him four of his companions, Mael Chróin, Mael Da Lua, Mael Shenaigh and Mac Deoraidh. His brother Muiredach used to visit him there, and did nothing without consulting him.[1] Guaire was suspicious of the ambitions of Muiredach and Cellach, and resolved upon Cellach's death. He invited him to a feast with intent to have him poisoned, but Cellach declined to leave his hermitage. The four disciples, however, went to Guaire, and were persuaded, with promises of land and riches and wives of their own choice, to murder Cellach. On their return the saint observed their changed aspect and divined their purpose. He pleaded with them against so evil an act, and they admitted their plan and persisted in it. They put Cellach into a boat and brought him to the mainland and into the forest. He besought them for a night's delay, and this was granted. Cellach was much afraid, and did not sleep; and he might have escaped, for the others slept, but he would not evade the will of God, and it seemed that they would overtake him anyway. When morning came, Cellach at first shut out the light in terror, and then reproached himself for lack of trust in God, and opened the door. Then he pronounced a lay:

'Hail to the bright morning as it comes into my cell, and hail to Him who sends it, triumphant morning, ever young.
'Daughter of the proud . . . , sister of the shining sun, I welcome the bright morning which lights my book for me.

.   .   .   .

'O scallcrow, grey bird with the pointed beak, I can tell from your behaviour that you are no friend to Cellach.
'O croaking raven, if you are hungry, do not depart from the mound until you eat of my flesh.
'The kite of the yew tree of Cluain Eo will be rough in the struggle: he will carry off the fill of his grey talons, he will not part from me kindly.
'The fox in the dark wood will come quickly at the sound

[1] So also Guaire consulted Marbán (p. 93) and Domnall consulted his brother Mael Chaba (p. 58).

of the blow: he will devour my flesh and blood in his cold and secret lair.

'The wolf from the mound to the east of Druim Mic Dair will come within an hour to be lord of the gentle pack.

'O Mael Chróin, you have resolved upon a wicked deed. The son of Eogan would not permit your death for twenty ounces of gold.

'O Mael Chróin, you do well to betray me: you have chosen your doom, you have chosen hell.

.   .   .   .

'May the Lord, the son of Holy Mary above, say to me: "you must have earth, you shall have Heaven; welcome awaits thee, Cellach."'

Then his four companions killed Cellach, and came before Guaire; and he received them with joy for their evil deed. And ravens and wolves and wild beasts came and ate of the saint's flesh as he had foretold. But every beast that ate of his flesh fell sick and died.

Muiredach discovered the body of his brother and brought it away for burial. Two wild deer came with a bier and bore the body to a church where the clerics received it. The wild deer remained there afterwards and ploughed like oxen and tended the saint's grave. But the friends of Cellach gathered to Muiredach,[1] and, as they were not strong enough to oppose Guaire, they went to Marcán, king of Hy Many, and stayed a year with him. At the end of that time he asked them to depart and visit Tara, as he was loath to offend Guaire further.

(670–859) Cú Choingelt and his men set out eastwards for Tara where Diarmait and Bláthmac, sons of Aed Sláine, reigned together. They were made welcome there, and Cú Choingelt was the guest of Bláthmac while his men were quartered about the country. Bláthmac had a daughter Aife, and she and Cú Choingelt loved each other. One day when Bláthmac and Cú Choingelt were playing chess, Aife showed her lover the move that won the game for him. Her father questioned her and she confessed her love. Cú Choingelt said that they had done no wrong together and waited upon his consent. Bláthmac gave his consent at

---

[1] His other name was Cú Choingelt, because he had slain a monster at the isthmus (*coingelt*) between Loch Conn and Loch Cullen (532–51).

once, and the lovers became man and wife. All was well for a
time, but one night Aife reproached her husband for his slow-
ness to avenge his brother's death.

On the next day, Cú Choingelt summoned his people and set
out for Connacht, in spite of the entreaties of Bláthmac and of
his wife. She foretold that he would be loved by the women of
Connacht and would never return to her, and lamented his
departure in a lay. They travelled into Tirawley, his own territory, and, having lodged his followers in a safe place, Cú
Choingelt set out in search of food. He came upon a herd of
swine, and killed a hog.[1] The swineherd warned him that he
would regret the deed, for the land on which he stood was the
estate of the four who had murdered Cellach, and it had been
granted them by Guaire.

'The swineherd was staring at the warrior. "If I mistake
not," said the swineherd, "you are Cú Choingelt son of
Eogan, though it is long since I saw you." "You are right,"
said Cú Choingelt. The lad put his arms about his neck and
gave him three kisses. "Do you know me?" said the swineherd. "Not yet," said Cú Choingelt. "I am the little acolyte
that you saw with Cellach, your brother, and God be thanked
that you came first to me in this country. Have you men
with you?"'

The swineherd provided food for all the company, and led
Cú Choingelt to the house where the four murderers were hold-
ing a feast for their inauguration as lords of the territory. He
went disguised, and ordered his men to follow. When all
within were drunk his men stormed the place and seized the
four usurpers. Their followers were slain before their eyes,
but Cú Choingelt bade the assembled guests continue the feast,
for he knew they were his friends. Next day the four were
taken out and their limbs were cut from their bodies while they
were still alive, and their bodies then hanged upon stout stakes,
so that they were thus put to death. And the place is named
Ard na Riag ('the hill of the gibbets').[2]

(860–914) Then Cú Choingelt went into Hy Fiachrach and
took hostages and assumed the lordship of that country, and his
honour and his fame were great, so that great as was the honour

---

[1] Cf. 'The Exile of Conall Corc', p. 37.   [2] s. Metr. Dinds. iii 414.

of Guaire, the poets preferred Cú Choingelt. Then he held
Tirawley and Hy Fiachrach, and Guaire held Hy Fiachrach
Aidne; and there was war between them so that both territories
were well nigh destroyed. But Geilgéis daughter of Guaire loved
Cú Choingelt, and at last peace was made and Geilgéis was given
to him as his wife. And the two rivals showed friendship to each
other, and the honour of Cú Choingelt was great throughout
Ireland.

Cú Choingelt was reconciled to Guaire's followers, but he
continued to plunder the churches of the country, and this dis-
pleased Guaire. And Guaire planned another act of treachery.
He sent St. Ciarán to Cú Choingelt with an invitation to come
for a settlement of peace, and the promise of the kingdom.
Ciarán urged him not to fail of the kingship through lack of trust
in Guaire; and Geilgéis urged him too, for she knew that Ciarán
was not treacherous, and she thought that Guaire would not
practice treachery against Ciarán. Cú Choingelt consented to
go with Ciarán against his inclination, for many were urging
him to it. He said:

'I am loath to go, although I go. Yet it is right to go,
whether I come safe or not.
'I saw an evil dream, the swine of the son of Colmán rend-
ing me: it will go ill with me if the dream comes true!
'I saw an evil dream, the swine of the son of Colmán rend-
ing me: I will not hesitate because of it, though I should be
going to my death.'

Then he went with Ciarán to Durlas, and they were entertained for three nights, and an alliance of friendship was made
between Guaire and Cú Choingelt in Ciarán's presence. Ciarán
departed, and Guaire resolved upon another murder, the slaying
of his kinsman, the husband of his daughter. And Guaire
accomplished that design so that Cú Choingelt was killed by him.

(The text is followed by a poem of twenty-nine quatrains on
the deserted home of Eogan Bél. It recounts the cursing of
Guaire by St. Ciarán, and the fall of his stronghold at Durlas.)

TROMDÁM GUAIRE
THE GREAT VISITATION TO GUAIRE

The tradition that the great saga *Táin Bó Cualnge* had been forgotten and was revealed to Senchán by the warrior Fergus, arisen from the grave, is preserved in various forms. They have been recorded and analysed by Thurneysen, *Heldensage* 251–67.[1] In one (RIA D 4.2)[2] it is simply said that Guaire asked Senchán to recite the *Táin* so as to test him with a difficult question, for it was a *geis* for a *fili* to be ignorant. And the account of the discovery is briefly told. The second[3] (Eg. 1782)[4] tells us more. Senchán with thrice fifty poets visited Guaire and was entertained by him for a year and a month, during which time the poets demanded various things difficult to obtain so as to dishonour him. But he was enabled by the favour of God and the assistance of the saintly swineherd Marbán to protect his honour and satisfy their desires. Then Marbán came to visit the poets in order to punish them for their exactions. He demanded of them that they recite the *Táin*. All were silent, and Marbán invoked heaven and earth and the curse of all the saints of Ireland if they spent two nights in the same place until they discovered the story of the *Táin*. They searched Ireland and Scotland in vain, and at last Saint Caillín,[5] a son of Senchán's mother, advised them to go to the grave of Fergus and make a triduum of prayer to the Lord that he raise the hero Fergus Mac Róich from the grave. They did so, and Fergus arose and recited the *Táin* to the poets. Senchán put it together and wrote it in a book.

There is a third recension in which the story of the poets' visitation is told at length. It is preserved in the Book of Lismore (fifteenth century) under the title *Tromdám Guaire*, and in later paper manuscripts, and it presents the complete text of which the second recension is a mere summary. The language of the Lismore text is, however, hardly earlier than the fourteenth century, while that of Eg. 1782 is certainly older, so that we must assume a common original. Thurneysen supposed (*Heldensage* 254) that the Lismore recension is a late story based upon the Egerton recension, but this seems to me most improbable. The Egerton recension has all the appearance of a brief synopsis of well-known tradition. The third recension is summarized here.

---

[1] In support of the tradition that the Táin was first committed to writing as early as the sixth century, s. Thurneysen, ZCP 19, 209.

[2] Ed. Meyer, ACL iii 4.

[3] Thurneysen's first recension is disregarded here, as Guaire is not concerned in it.   [4] Ed. Meyer, ACL iii 3.

[5] The name is illegible in the MS., but appears in *Tromdám Guaire* 1241.

Ed. Maud Joynt, Med. and Mod. Ir. Series ii (Lism. with variant readings); an earlier edition by Owen Connellan, also from the Book of Lismore, under the title *Imtheacht na Tromdháimhe, Trans. Oss. Soc.* v (Dublin, 1860), includes a translation. Numbers refer to the lines of Miss Joynt's edition.

(1–44) Aed son of Dua the Black was king of Oriel, and Aed the Fair son of Fergna was king of Bréifne; and these two were rivals, one seeking always to surpass the other in every matter. And they were not alike, for Aed the Fair was wealthy and successful, and Aed son of Dua the Black was warlike and contentious. The king of Oriel had a shield, Duibgilla, which made the enemy who beheld it in battle as weak as a woman after childbirth, so that every battle was a victory for him who bore it, even though he were alone against an army. Echaid Rígéices who was known also as Dallán Forgaill[1] was once on a visit with the king of Bréifne, and the king boasted of his generosity to the poet and argued that his rival, the king of Oriel, ought to show him equal favour. He then offered Dallán a hundred of each kind of cattle if he would go to the king of Oriel and demand the magic shield.

(45–203) Dallán set out with thrice nine *ollams* in his train and was made welcome. He asked for the shield, but the king answered that it was not a fitting request for a man of learning. Dallán recited a poem in praise of Aed which he had composed in order to win the shield. (The poem is in the obscure *bérla na filed*, and Dallán explains it in plain language to the king.) The king offered him a reward in money and cattle. Dallán recited two more poems in the same obscure form,[2] and the king offered him rich rewards, but he would accept only the shield. This the king refused, and Dallán threatened to satirize him. The king invoked the protection of God against his satire, and reminded him that when the saints of Ireland made peace between the kings and the poets (at the Assembly of Druim Cett), it was agreed that if a poet used his power of satire unjustly the shameful blotches would appear not on the face of his victim but upon his own face. He named the saints

---

[1] They are different persons in the preface to *Amra Choluimb Chille*, RC 20, 42. 18.

[2] The second of these poems echoes passages of the poem attributed to Dallán which is preserved separately in LL (193 b 34) and H.3.18, ed. Connellan from H.3.18, *Trans. Oss. Soc.* v 258.

concerned,[1] but Dallán declared that all these saints would not
avail to protect him, and proceeded to satirize him. He then
explained the satire in plain language as before. Aed dismissed
him, and on his way from the place Dallán miraculously recovered his sight. He recognized that as a warning of death,
and asked to be taken to his house. After three days he died.

(203–85) The poets then assembled to elect a chief, and
Senchán was chosen to succeed Dallán. He composed an elegy
on Dallán and was acknowledged a worthy successor. Then the
poets debated as to where they should go on a visitation, and
Senchán proposed that they should visit Guaire son of Colmán,
for he had never been satirized for refusing gold or treasure.
All agreed to follow Senchán's advice. Guaire made preparations to receive them. A house was built for their comfort with
eight sides: eight beds were placed along each side, and a lower
bed in front of each of them. He dug wells for the men and
separate wells for the women,[2] and collected provisions for their
entertainment. Then he sent messengers to invite them. But
Senchán said that he would not bring his whole company lest
it should be too much of a burden on the province of Connacht,
so he brought only a hundred and fifty poets, a hundred and
fifty minor poets, a hundred and fifty hounds, a hundred and
fifty servants, a hundred and fifty women, and three times nine
of every craft.[3] And that number came to Durlas.

(286–459) Guaire made them welcome and lodged them in the
great house. Food was put before them, and the king told them
only to ask for anything they wished and they would get it. But
that proved difficult, for they never lay down at night without
grumbling, nor arose without some one of them demanding
some extraordinary thing. First Muirenn, the wife of Dallán,
was seized with longing and uttered a groan. Senchán asked
what troubled her, and she said that if her desire was not satisfied she would die. She required a bowl of new milk with the
marrow of a wild pig's trotter; a pet cuckoo singing on a tree
beside her, although it was then between Christmas and Little
Christmas; a full load of the lard of a white boar tied on her
back; a roan horse to ride on, and a cloak made of spiders'

---

[1] The list is almost identical with that in *Fled Dúin na nGéd* (p. 61).
[2] In the morning people washed themselves at a well or in a stream,
s. *Heldensage* 82.   [3] Here of course the author's satire begins.

webs; and that she might so ride into Durlas humming a tune.

In the morning Guaire came as usual to inquire for their welfare. Senchán told him that they were never in a worse plight than at that moment, and informed him of the longing that had come upon Muirenn. Guaire thought that this was not a matter of a single desire but of many unruly desires, the easiest of which was hard to provide. He despaired at first of supplying them, but prayed to God for help. Next day Marbán the Swineherd came to visit him. He was a son of Guaire's mother, and chose to herd swine so that he might lead a life of sanctity in the wilderness. Guaire told him his trouble, and Marbán advised him how all that had been asked for could be found. But the lard of the white boar could be had only by killing Marbán's pet boar, an animal that had served him faithfully, and for that demand Marbán vowed vengeance on the poets, and especially on her who required it. He said that he would come one day to visit them in order to avenge this wrong so that the poets would regret it for ever. When the wishes of Muirenn had been satisfied and she was riding upon the horse, humming a tune, the horse fell and she was injured so that she died. Hence the proverb: 'a hag's load of lard'.

(460–519) Medb, the daughter of Senchán was seized with longing and uttered a groan. Her desire was for abundance of blackberries, and it was the end of winter; that she should be on her way to Durlas, and that she should find Guaire's household stricken by disease when she arrived. Senchán asked her why she wished harm to Guaire who was entertaining them so well, and she replied that she was like the nettle, which stings the hand that protects it. With the help of Marbán her wishes were satisfied.

(520–800) (The series of unreasonable demands will not here be followed further, nor the exaggerated satire upon Senchán: how he refused to eat of the marvellous feast which was provided by Marbán to satisfy his unruly desire, and insulted those whom Guaire sent with special dainties to persuade him; how he satirized the mice for eating an egg that had been offered to him, and then the cats for not watching the mice. In a ludicrous passage the king of the cats comes to avenge the satire, and carries off the poet on his back; but as they are passing by the forge at Clonmacnoise, Saint Ciarán happens to be there and throws a piece of red-hot iron at the cat, killing it and thus delivering Senchán. He curses the hand that saved him, because he would rather have died so that the poets might have the opportunity of satirizing Guaire on account of his death.)

(801–1003) At last Marbán came to avenge the death of his pet boar as he had promised. He entered the poets' house not by the open door, away from the wind, but by the closed door to windward so that all within felt the draught of air. They rose in indignation and Senchán asked who this might be who had come in 'against the wind'. Marbán said it was an ignorant phrase, for he had come with the wind and brought plenty of it along with him.

'"You are come for a disputation," said Senchán. "Yes," said Marbán, "if I may have it?" "How then," said Senchán, "did it first arise?" "From the Nuts of Segais,"[1] said Marbán. "True," said Senchán, "and are you Marbán the Swineherd, chief prophet of heaven and earth?" "I am he," said Marbán. "What brings you here?" said Senchán. "I have heard," said Marbán, "that a man can find here any sort of music or of minstrelsy that he chooses, and I come to ask minstrelsy of you." "You shall have it," said Senchán, "if you are scholar's kin." "I am," said Marbán, "for the grandmother of my servant's wife was descended from a poet." "You shall have your choice of minstrelsy," said Senchán, "although the kinship is remote. What minstrelsy do you desire?" "There is none I should rather have just now," said Marbán, "than humming." "That is the easiest to provide," said Senchán.'

But the form of humming that Marbán required was that called *crónán snagach* which was apparently very exhausting. The hummers, twenty-seven in number, were brought before Marbán, and were soon prostrate. Marbán demanded the humming that was promised. Dael Duiled, the *ollam* of Leinster, got up, and offered another form of entertainment. He was a master of the art of question and answer, and asked Marbán what good thing Man found on earth that God did not find; which are the two trees whose foliage does not fall till they die;

---

[1] These were nuts from the nine hazels of wisdom which grew over the well of Segais, where the river Boyne rises, s. Metr. Dinds. index s.v. Segais.

what beast lives in the sea and is drowned when it is taken out
of it; what animal lives in fire and is burnt when it is taken out.
Marbán answered the questions: what Man found on earth that
God did not find was a worthy master; the two trees are the
holly and the yew; the beast that drowns when taken from the
sea is called *Gním Abraein*; that which is burnt when taken
out of the fire was first called *Tegillus* and is now called Sala-
mander. Dael Duiled threw himself upon the protection of
Marbán and retired from the contest.

One after the other the poets rose to challenge Marbán in
one branch or another of their art, but he overcame them in
turn, and persisted in demanding the humming he had first
requested. Finally Senchán himself offered to hum for him,
and Marbán said that he would take more pleasure in that than
if any other should perform. Senchán raised his beard into the
air and set about humming the *crónán snagach*. Whenever he
stopped Marbán said he was not yet satisfied. And at last with
the strain of his effort to hum, one of Senchán's eyes leaped
from its socket on to his cheek. Marbán now feared the displeasure of Guaire, so he said a prayer into his right hand, and
the eye was restored to its place. And then he asked for more
humming.

(1004–26) 'One in the house said: "I shall make minstrelsy
for you, Marbán." "Who are you," said Marbán, "and what
is the minstrelsy?" "I am the best storyteller in the Great
Visitation," said he, "and in all Ireland, and Fis son of
Fochmhairc[1] is my name." "If you are the best storyteller
in Ireland," said Marbán, "you know the chief stories of
Ireland." "I do indeed," said the storyteller. "Then," said
Marbán, "tell me *Táin Bó Cualnge*." The storyteller was
silent and blushed for shame. "Why do you not tell the story
to Marbán?" said Senchán. "By your leave, royal *ollam*,"
said the storyteller, "I have never heard that *Táin* told in
Ireland, and I know not who has told it." "Well," said
Marbán, "I put you under *gesa* until you tell me the *Táin*,
and I put all the Great Visitation under *gesa* if they stay two
nights in the same house until they discover the *Táin*. And
by the grace of God I take from you all the gift of poetry, so

---

[1] 'Knowledge son of Enquiry.'

that you shall not make a single stanza save one poem only,
until you get for me *Táin Bó Cualnge*. And now I leave you,"
said Marbán, "and on my word, if it were not for Guaire, I
would dearly avenge the white boar upon you, you inconstant
ignorant poets!"'

(1027–1275) Marbán departed and left the poets in dismay.
Senchán announced that they must set out at once in search
of the *Táin* in order to abide by the *gesa* that had been laid
upon them. They went first to take leave of Guaire, and he
begged them to stay even though they could no longer practise
their art. But Senchán rejected the bounty of mere charity.
Guaire asked them to leave at least the women and children and
servants with him, and they consented. Senchán bestowed upon
Guaire the one poem that they were free to make, and in four
stanzas he recited the hospitality the poets had enjoyed for the
year and four months that they were there.

The poets set out for Naas, the dwelling of the king of
Leinster, so that they might proceed to Scotland in search of
the *Táin*. On their way they met a leper who spoke harshly to
them, saying that their coming into a country was a misfortune
and their departure a blessing. He asked where they were
going, and warned them that they had no right to visit the king
of Leinster while they were without the gift of poetry. They
tried to compose a poem, each *ollam* attempting a single stanza,
but they were unable to put the words in order. The leper then
offered to make a poem for them upon one condition, namely
that Senchán would give him a kiss. Senchán refused, but the
other poets threatened to abandon him, and he was forced to
consent. Thus was fulfilled a malediction pronounced by Guaire
against Senchán in the course of his unruly behaviour.

The king received them kindly, and the leper recited a poem
for them. On the next day they were given a boat, and they
sailed for Scotland. When they came near the Isle of Man they
saw a person seated upon a cliff above them, and he forbade
them to land unless they could match verses with him.[1] The
leper was in the prow of the boat and was able to complete each
of the three half-quatrains that the figure uttered. He told
them that it was a woman-doctor who had addressed them.

[1] Cf. p. 45, note 1.

Half the year she practised healing and the other half she spent making salt. She had stored a fortune of sixty marks of which she would give half to the poets to provide for their stay in Scotland. Then the leper vanished. It happened as he had foretold, and the poets sailed on to Scotland where they were received by the royal *ollam* of Scotland, Mael Gedic son of Fer Goboch, and they spent the night with him. That was the best night that they spent in Scotland.

The poets searched Scotland, north, south, east and west, for a whole year, and found no trace of the *Táin*. At last Senchán decided to return to Ireland, and they embarked in their boat and sailed to Áth Cliath[1] where they were met by Saint Caillín, a son of Senchán's mother. He told them that he was the leper whom Senchán had been forced to kiss. Senchán appealed to him for help, and Caillín replied that they must return to Durlas and send for Marbán, for he alone knew where the *Táin* could be found.

Saint Caillín went with Senchán and the other poets to Durlas, where Guaire received them kindly, and they sent for Marbán. He told them that no one living or dead could tell the story of the *Táin* save one man only, namely Fergus Mac Róich, for he alone knew the deeds of the men of Ireland and of the men of Ulster on the *Táin*, and it was on his account that that expedition was made. He bade them summon the saints of Ireland and go with them to the grave of Fergus, and there to fast upon the Lord for three days and three nights so that Fergus might be sent to recite the *Táin* to them.

(1276–1316) 'Caillín went and brought the saints of Ireland to Durlas, and they spent a night there feasting. And on the morrow they went to the grave of Fergus, and they were praying to Jesus Christ to send Fergus to them. And he wished to stand as he recited the *Táin* to them, but they could hear nothing of it from him until they made him sit down. And he recited the *Táin* to them in that way. And he that wrote it down from him was Ciarán of Clonmacnoise, and the place in which he wrote it was upon the hide of the Dun Cow. Fergus recited the story until at length he had finished it, and he went back into the same grave. And the

[1] The site of the city of Dublin.

saints gave thanks to God that they had received their
petition from Him about the question that Senchán had asked
them, through the powers of the saints of Ireland and the
advice of Marbán the Swineherd. These are the saints that
came there: Colum Cille son of Feidlim, and Saint Caillín and
Ciarán of Clonmacnoise and Old Ciarán of Saigir and Findén
of Clonard, Findén of Moville, Seanach son of Gaitre, Brendan
of Birr and Brendan son of Findlug.'[1]

The saints and the poets returned to Durlas and spent a night
there feasting. The poets asked Marbán to come that the *Táin*
might be recited to him, and he said that he would come only
if they would abide by the judgement that he would pronounce
upon them. They promised to abide by it. Then Marbán came
and the story of the *Táin* was told to him, and he restored the
gift of poetry to Senchán and to the poets. Marbán then
brought them to his own house and entertained them for a
week. He asked for his right of judgement as they had promised,
and made the poets give the saints of Ireland as sureties.

'"The judgement that I pronounce on you," said Marbán,
"is that each *ollam* shall return to his own territory and that
there shall be no Great Visitation in future." And each *ollam*
went to his own territory at the instance of Marbán and the
saints of Ireland, and the Great Visitation travelled no more
in Ireland ever since. *Finit*.'

[1] Cf. the similar list of saints on p. 61.

FERGAL SON OF MAEL DÚIN, A.D. 709–22

FERGAL became king of Ireland in 709, according to the Annals of Ulster, and was killed in the battle of Allen in 722 (AU 721).[1] Cathal son of Findguine was king of Cashel and died in 742 (AU 741). He figures in 'The Vision of Mac Con Glinne', and is cured of gluttony when Mac Con Glinne banishes the demon who has possessed him. The devastation of Mag Breg by Cathal and an invasion of Leinster by Fergal to levy the *Bórama* and take hostages are recorded *s.a.* 720 (= 721). These events introduce the story of the battle of Allen, which is the only saga about Fergal that has been preserved.

CATH ALMAINE

THE BATTLE OF ALLEN

The saga is contained in YBL (fcs. 206a9), the Book of Fermoy (p. 128, 15th century) and in a seventeenth-century Brussels manuscript. It is not a particularly good example of its kind, but it has some interesting features, notably the episode of the singing head, §§ 19–22, to which may be compared the head of Bendigeit Vran in the Welsh story *Branwen ferch Llyr*, which entertained the assembled company at Gwales for eighty years (WB 30a19–29 = Loth, *Les Mabinogion* i 145, 149), and the honouring of the head of Fergal (§ 26).

No study of the date of the text or of the relationship of the three manuscripts has yet been made. The language of YBL is Middle Irish and may perhaps be assigned to the eleventh or early twelfth century.

Ed. with translation, O'Donovan, *Annals of Ireland. Three Fragments* 32–51 (Brussels 5301–20); Stokes, RC 24, 41 (YBL with variants from F and B). The numbers indicate the paragraphs of Stokes's edition.

(1–2) Cathal son of Findguine and Fergal son of Mael Dúin were at war for a long time. Fergal plundered the Leinstermen to vex Cathal,[2] and Cathal wasted the whole of Mag Breg.

---

[1] There is an error of one year in the Annals of Ulster from 712 (*recte* 713) to 1012 (*recte* 1013), s. Paul Walsh, *Irish Historical Studies* ii 369.

[2] Leinster appears here as the ally, perhaps a dependent ally, of the kingdom of Cashel.

Then they made peace. But Fergal came again into Leinster
to exact the *Bórama*, and he brought with him the men of the
north.[1] He had been assembling his army for a long time, and
each man would say: 'I shall go with you if Donn Bó goes
with you.'

(3) Donn Bó was the son of a widow, and he was the noblest,
fairest boy in Ireland. His mother refused to let him go unless
the guarantees and pledges of Colum Cille[2] were given him for
his safe return, and this was done.

(4–8) Fergal then advanced into Leinster, but the expedition
started badly. His guides led him astray, and a leper whose hut
was close to where they pitched their camp was outraged by the
men and foretold the vengeance of the Lord upon the Uí Néill.
Fergal called upon Donn Bó to entertain the camp that night,
for he was the best entertainer in Ireland with stories and poetry
and music; but he could not recite. Ua Maiglinni, the chief
jester of Ireland, recited in his stead, and told the battles and
triumphs of Leth Cuinn and Leinster from the Destruction of
Dinn Ríg down to that time. The men slept little that night
for fear of the Leinstermen, and because of the great storm; for
it was the eve of St. Findén.[3]

(9–15) The Leinstermen came to meet Fergal and the battle
was joined, and it was the fiercest that ever was fought in
Ireland till then. Colum Cille did not aid the Uí Néill,[4] for he
saw Brigid above the Leinster army terrifying the army of Leth
Cuinn. It was indeed the sight of her that caused the defeat
of Fergal by Aed, king of North Leinster. Fergal himself and
Buan son of Baile, king of Scotland, were slain by Aed, and
Donn Bó too was killed. Here are given the names of the kings
of the Northern and Southern Uí Néill who fell in the battle.

[1] i.e. The Northern Uí Néill. Fergal belonged to the Southern Uí Néill.

[2] B interprets this to mean that Maol son of Failbhe, a coarb of Colum
Cille, should guarantee his safe return. Does this mean simply that he should
pledge the reputation of Colum Cille as a mediator of supernatural favours?
No technical meaning can here be attached to *rátha* and *cora*, but they are
legal terms. For *ráth* 'guarantee, surety', s. Thurneysen, *Bürgschaft* 35–56.
The looser use of *cor* in the literature is referred to, *ib*. 83. I have not found
the name of Maol son of Failbhe in the annals.

[3] i.e. the 11th of December.

[4] He was himself one of them, and the *Cathach* ('Battle Shrine') of the
O'Donnells, which was carried into battle by that branch of the family, con-
tained a manuscript probably written by him, and now preserved in the Royal
Irish Academy.

Nine kings were seized with frenzy (like the famous Suibne). The battle was fought on Tuesday, the third of the Calends of December.[1]

(16–19) Ua Maiglinni was killed by the Leinstermen, and Aed Allán, king of Hy Many, who besought his sons to save him, was also taken and slain. Then, at night, when the Leinstermen were feasting, Murchad son of Bran offered seven *cumals* as reward to anyone who would bring in a man's head from the battlefield. Baethgalach went out and came to where Fergal's body lay. He heard a voice bidding the musicians entertain their king Fergal, even though he and they had fallen. Then wonderful music was heard, and there was one voice that was sweeter than any other. It was the voice of the head of Donn Bó. When the warrior approached, the head bade him come no farther, for it was pledged to sing for Fergal that night, and not for Murchad. 'Where is Fergal?' said the warrior. 'That fair corpse beyond you is he', said the head.

(20–3) The warrior returned to the house with the head and placed it upon a pillar. All the company recognized the head of Donn Bó and lamented his death, saying that he was the best musician in Ireland. Then the warrior called upon the head for Christ's sake, into Whose presence it had gone,[2] to sing for the Leinstermen as he had sung for Fergal before. The head turned its face to the wall so that it might be in the dark, and then it sang aloud and so sweetly that all the company wept at the sadness of the music that it sang. When they were weary of their sadness in listening to that music, the warrior brought the head back to where the corpse lay. 'Join my head to my body', said the head. The warrior fitted the head to the body and it adhered to it straight away, in fulfilment of the word of Colum Cille, promising that Donn Bó should return safely to his mother. Thus the news of the battle and of Fergal's death was told to her and to everyone.

(24–6) The Leinstermen had fought this battle of Allen without the consent of Cathal son of Findguine, and Cathal was angry at that. When the Leinstermen heard of his displeasure,

[1] i.e. Tuesday, 29th of November. This must be an error. The Annals of Tigernach and AU agree on the date Friday the 11th of December, which fits the year 722, s. *Irish Historical Studies* ii 369.

[2] What is meant is, of course, that the soul of Donn Bó was in the presence of Christ, and the warrior is addressing Donn Bó.

they resolved to bring the head of Fergal to Cathal for a common triumph. So it was done, and Fergal's poet Rumann sang:

'Fergal is slain, a handsome man now full of wounds, fierce in deeds of enmity: one wail like thunder sounds from Clew Bay to the Isle of Man.'

Cathal was in Glendamain of the Kings at Sliab Crot; and he tried to kill those who brought him the head, for he was angry that Fergal had been killed in violation of the peace that had been made between them.[1] He ordered the head to be washed and combed and dressed in a satin cloth. Seven oxen and seven wethers and seven pigs were cooked and placed before Fergal's head. The head blushed in the presence of the Munstermen, and opened its eyes to God to give thanks for the reverence and great honour that had been shown it. The food was then distributed to the poor of the neighbouring churches.

(27) Then Cathal went with a chosen company of the Munstermen to convey the head of Fergal, and he brought it himself to the Uí Néill. He gave the kingship[2] of the Uí Néill to Flaithbeartach son of Aed. After six weeks Cathal returned to Glendamain of the Kings.

(28–9) Afterwards a great war against Cathal broke out in Leinster, and Cathal mustered the Munstermen and marched against Faelán, king of Leinster, who was supported by all the Leinstermen. Then the battle of Fele was fought between Faelán and Cathal, in which Faelchar, king of Ossory, was killed and the Leinstermen were defeated. That is the story of the feud between Cathal and the Leinstermen.

---

[1] The Leinstermen were therefore bound by that agreement. Cf. p. 99, note 2.

[2] A curious statement. The king was not appointed by a stranger, but chosen, at least in theory, by the people, from among those of royal blood. Least of all should we expect the king of Cashel to appoint the High King. The emendation of *tarad* to *tartad* would give the sense: 'the kingship was given.'

BÓRAMA

THE TRIBUTE

There is one remarkable story which cannot properly be assigned to a particular cycle, as it extends through a long period of time. Its literary merit is offset by its lack of form, for it consists of a succession of episodes loosely strung together. The theme is the famous tribute called *Bórama* which was exacted from Leinster by the Uí Néill for many centuries, and was the occasion of numerous battles from the time of its alleged imposition by Tuathal Techtmar (†A.D. 76) until its remission by Finnachta at the instance of Saint Mo Ling in the seventh century.[1] Between the episodes the author inserts mere lists of names of kings who exacted the tribute, or who failed to exact it, so that the text appears to be a compilation of incidents connected with the tribute, into which these names have been introduced in order to present a complete record. The chief episode, making about half the text, is the story of the battle of Belach Dúin Bolg (A.D. 594) in the reign of Aed son of Ainmire.[2] Within this story is an interpolation about Saint Colum Cille (§§ 95–104) which is quite irrelevant.

The text is preserved in LL (fcs. 294b25–308b49) but there is a longer recension, in the Book of Lecan (fcs. 295a24–310a12). The question of its date has not been investigated, nor has that of its sources, but the language is early Middle Irish. In its present form it may go back to the tenth or eleventh century. The Lecan text has not been published, and it seems to be much better than that in LL.

Ed. with translation Stokes, RC 13, 32–124 (LL with readings from Lecan, omitting many verse passages); O'Grady, SG i 359–90 = ii 401–24 (LL; the verse is included in the text, but not in the translation). Numbers in brackets refer to paragraphs of Stokes's edition.

(1–13) Tuathal Techtmar son of Fiacha Findfolaid son of Feradach Findfechtnach became king of Ireland when he routed the vassal tribes of Ulster, Leinster, Munster and Connacht who had slain his father and his grandfather in the Revolt of the Vassals. He settled at Tara and celebrated the Feast of Tara;

---

[1] In 693 according to the *Annals of Clonmacnoise*, p. 54. The incident is not recorded in FM, nor in Tigernach, but the latter quotes a stanza attributed to Mo Ling which refers to it, RC 17, 213.

[2] O'Donovan gives a summary of this part of the text in a long footnote, FM i 218, note h. It is preserved independently in YBL (fcs. 207b37). Cf. Plummer, *Lives of Irish Saints* ii 223, §§ 139–141 = VSH ii 161 § lv.

and the people of Ireland, men and women, boys and girls, there gave all the Elements as surety that they would never contest the kingship against him or his descendants. The provincial kings who were present at that feast were Fergus Febail, king of Ulster, Eogan son of Ailill Érand, king of Cú Roi's province, Eochu son of Dáire, king of the province of Eochu Mac Luchtai, Conrach son of Derg, king of Connacht, and Eochu son of Eochu Domlén, king of Leinster.[1]

Tuathal had two daughters, Fithir and Dáirine, and the king of Leinster took Fithir, the elder, to wife, for it was not then the custom for the younger to wed before the elder. But when he returned home to Ráith Immil, his people said that he had left the better girl behind. He returned to Tara and said that Fithir was dead, and asked for Dáirine. When Fithir saw Dáirine arrive as a second wife, she died of shame, and Dáirine died of grief at her sister's death. Then the two bodies were washed[2] at Áth Toncha ('ford of washing') and people said: 'grievous (garb) is the washing', whence the place is called Garbthonach.

When Tuathal learned the truth he sent the news to the king of Connacht, who was foster-father to Fithir, and to the king of Ulster, who was foster-father to Dáirine, and they came with their armies to assist him. The three armies, twenty-two thousand men, advanced against Leinster, and the Leinstermen advanced to meet them. The first encounter was with the men of Ulster, and Fergus Febail was slain, but his army was successful and burnt Naas and Alenn and destroyed Bárc Bresail, a wooden fortress built by Bresal Brathirchend, High King of the world. Then the Leinstermen, nine thousand strong, gave battle at Ráith Immil which is now called Garbthonach, and Eochu, king of Leinster, was killed, and twenty kings along with him. All through the autumn the men of Ireland harried Leinster, and at last the Leinstermen agreed to pay the eric for the death of Tuathal's daughters, and Erc son of Eochu Domlén was allowed to remain king of Leinster.

This is the eric: thrice five thousand cows, thrice five thou-

---

[1] The five provinces here are Ulster, South Munster, North Munster, Connacht, and Leinster, cf. p. 60, note 2.

[2] So the body of Muirchertach son of Erc († 526) was washed in the Boyne, RC 23, 424, § 43.

sand swine, thrice five thousand mantles, thrice five thousand
silver chains, thrice five thousand wethers, thrice five thousand
copper cauldrons, a great cauldron of copper which held twelve
swine and twelve oxen for the house of Tara itself, thirty white
cows with red ears, with calves of the same colour, with ties
and tethers of bronze, and bronze pails as well.[1]

(14–21) (Now we are given the names of seven kings after
Tuathal who levied the Tribute, although it is said of the fifth,
who was Art son of Conn, that 'he levied it not without battles'.)

(22–36) Then Cairpre Lifechar became king of Ireland and
demanded the Tribute, but Bressal Bélach,[2] king of Leinster,
said that he would fight rather than pay it, and went for aid
to Find son of Cumall.[3] Find and his warriors set out northwards along the Barrow. When they reached the point of Ros
mBrocc, Find sat down on a high ridge and he beheld angels
ascending and descending in the sky. He foretold the coming
of the Christian monks. Then Mo Ling the Swift, a foster-
brother to Find, came up to them. He advised Find not to set
his small force against the army of the men of Ireland. They
all went to Mo Ling's dwelling and feasted there for three days
and three nights, and while they were there a champion named
Énán had a vision in which he saw St. Mo Ling and his com-
munity.[4] (In a short poem he tells the vision and places himself
under the protection of the saint, 'helmsman of truth'.) Meanwhile the *fiana* of Ireland assembled from every quarter, and
Find then led them to Garbthonach, and from there on the
morrow to meet the army of the Gailiáin (the Leinstermen).
The two armies advanced against the northern force as far as
Cnámross, and there a battle was fought in which the Leinstermen were victorious. The men of Ireland were routed, nine
thousand of them were slain including Cairpre Lifechar's three
sons, Eochu, Eochu Domlén, and Fiacha Roptene.

(37) From that time forth the Tribute was not levied from
Leinster until the thirty princesses, and a hundred maidens
with each of them, were slain at Tara by Dúnlang son of Énna

---

[1] A different version of the amount of the Tribute is given, *Annals of
Clonmacnoise*, p. 53.

[2] He was a son of Fiacha Bacced son of the famous Cathaer Már, and died
in 435 (FM).   [3] The hero of the Fenian Cycle.

[4] The place was afterwards the site of St. Mo Ling's foundation, s. FM i 298,
note x.

Niae, from which deed the Crooked Mound in Tara has its
name. Then the Tribute was again laid upon Leinster.[1]

(38–42) After that the Leinstermen were victorious in many
battles against Eochu Muigmedón and Niall of the Nine
Hostages in withholding the Tribute. And then Loegaire son
of Niall became king of Ireland, and he too was defeated in an
attempt to enforce it at the battle of Áth Dara (FM 457). His
army was routed and he himself taken captive, so that he was
forced to swear by the Elements never to demand the Tribute
again. After two years and a half he again raided Leinster, but
he perished, a victim of the Elements which he had defied.

(There follows a list of forty-five battles in which the Leinstermen successfully resisted the claim. The kings of Ireland named
are Ailill Molt, Lugaid son of Loegaire and Diarmait son of
Cerball. 'Though the kings of Tara used to exact the *Bórama*,
many of them used to take it only by force.')

(43–55) Aed son of Ainmire became king of Ireland.[2] He had
four sons, Domnall, Mael Choba the cleric, Gabrán and Cummascach. Cummascach set out on a 'free circuit' of Ireland so
that he might enjoy the privilege of a night with the wife of
every king in Ireland. He went into Leinster with four battalions. Brandub son of Eochu was then king of Leinster, and
he resolved upon an act of treachery. He let it be said that he
had gone abroad to levy tribute from the Britons, and billeted
the guests throughout the country with orders that they should
all be killed. After Cummascach had arrived, Brandub disguised himself as a slave and helped to prepare a feast. Cummascach asked where the queen was, and she was brought to
him. He asked a boon of her, that she should spend the night
with him. She asked a boon of him, that he should not detain
her until she had finished serving her guests so that she might
'purchase her honour from them'.[3] He consented, and she went
away and took refuge in the secret shelter of Buchet's House.

---

[1] This is recorded in FM *s.a.* 241, in the reign of Cormac, father of Cairpre,
so that the compiler of the text has gone astray here. There is no mention
in the Annals of the battle described above. Perhaps § 37 should be transferred
to follow § 21 of Stokes's edition.

[2] *Annals of Tigernach*, RC 17, 149 = FM 568. Here the Lecan text is at
fcs. 305d22, but it does not begin here as Stokes imagined.

[3] The phrase is not clear to me. Would she, by showing herself a queen
through her hospitality, justify to her guests the granting of the favour which
Cummascach asked, and which was apparently due from the king's wife?

Then Glasdám, the satirist of the King of Ireland's Son, came
to ask for provisions. Brandub thrust the fork into the cauldron
and brought up nine joints with a single thrust. The satirist
exclaimed: 'It is the gift not of a slave but of a king!' He
brought the food to the house where Cummascach was, and
said the same to him.

Then Brandub brought a load of food into the house and set
it down before the King of Ireland's Son, and went out closing
the great door behind him. Four fires were set to the house, one
at each side.[1] Cummascach called out: 'Who is attacking the
house?' 'I,' said Brandub. Glasdám the satirist then said that
no treachery should be played against him for he had eaten
of Brandub's food. Brandub bade him climb up the wall and
leap from the roof over the fire, and he might go free. The
satirist gave his clothes to Cummascach, and in that way
Cummascach escaped. He was badly hurt, but he made his way
to Móin Cummascaig at Cell Rannairech.[2] There he met
Lóchine Lond, ancestor of the O'Lonans and erenagh of Cell
Rannairech, who cut off his head and brought it to Brandub.[3]

(56–119) Aedán, bishop of Glendalough, a son of the mother
of Aed son of Ainmire, came to visit Brandub, and advised him
to send messengers to Ailech, where Aed dwelt, to announce
that his son had been killed for his misdeeds.[4] The messengers
brought the news to Aed who informed them that he knew it
already. He sent them away unharmed, but said that he would
follow them.

Then Aed assembled a great army and marched against
Leinster to avenge the death of Cummascach and to levy the
Tribute which had been paid by the Leinstermen to the descen-
dants of Conn from the time of Tuathal Techtmar till then.
Brandub was in the south of Uí Chendsalaig, and he came
northwards to Belach Dubthaire, which is now called Belach
Con Glaise,[5] to his own dwelling. Bishop Aedán came to Brandub

[1] For the burning house cf. *sup.*, p. 6.
[2] Kilranelagh, near Baltinglass, County Wicklow.
[3] The slaying of Cummascach is recorded in the *Annals of Tigernach*, RC 17,
160 = FM 593. There he is said to have been killed at Buchet's House by
Brandub himself.
[4] This perhaps supports the probability of the existence of another version
according to which Cummascach pursued the queen to Buchet's House, and
was there taken and killed. His 'misdeeds' are not made clear in the story here.
[5] Baltinglass, County Wicklow.

and said that Aed was encamped at Dún Buacci. Brandub asked him to go and seek a truce so that he might gather his army. Aedán went to Aed and was made welcome. He asked for a truce. 'You shall not get that truce until you put your hand to the three members with which you make your children.'[1] Aedán was angered by this and said: 'If God knows me, may a she-wolf take your three members to yonder hill!' And so it happened. Aed advanced, taking Aedán along with him, and Aedán foretold disaster for him on the way. Aed pitched his camp at Cell Bélat,[2] and Aedán went on to visit Brandub. Brandub asked his advice, and the bishop said: 'Set a great royal torch outside on the rampart of this fort, and bring together three hundred teams, each of twelve oxen. Put white baskets upon them with many warriors in the baskets and straw over them, and food upon the straw. Get a hundred and fifty unbroken horses and tie bags to their tails filled with stones so as to frighten the horses of the men of Ireland. Let the great torch be before you with the royal cauldron about it until you shall reach the middle of the camp of the men of Ireland. Send messengers meanwhile to the king of Ireland and say that the food of Leinster will be brought to him to-night.' Brandub followed his advice.

(73–4) While these preparations were being made, Brandub set out with Aedán to observe the enemy. He had six-score warriors, and one horse on which he rode himself. The bishop was in a chariot. From a height they looked down upon the camp, and the bishop saw what seemed like flocks of birds of many colours motionless over the camp. Brandub explained that these were the banners of the army. The cleric spoke a lay in which he foretold the defeat of Aed, and praised the glories of Leinster and the valour of Brandub. Then he departed to Glendalough.

(75–8) Brandub and his men took the boys of Ulster by surprise and held them as hostages. The men of Ulster heard this and came seven thousand seven hundred strong, lay and cleric, and parleyed with Brandub. The king of Ulster agreed to make peace, and said that this friendship had been foretold by Conchobor Mac Nessa. He recites the poem in which Conchobor

---

[1] This seems to be a sign of submission, but I have no other example.
[2] Kilbaylet, near Donard, County Wicklow.

had told a vision of his own people and the men of Leinster drinking from a vat a mixture of blood, milk, and wine.[1] 'The holy men of Leinster and Ulster sat down on the mountain and made their covenant never to be broken.'

(82) Brandub went on horseback to challenge the men of Ireland, and the champion who came to meet him was Bláthach, and he was mounted on the king's own horse. Brandub struck off his head and departed, leading the king's horse in triumph.

(83–94) Then a spy was sent into Aed's camp, namely Rón Cerr son of Dubánach son of the king of Uí Mail. Calf's blood and rye-dough were rubbed on him, and he took a cowl and a wallet, so that he was like a leper. A wooden leg was given him, and he put his knee into the socket. And he went into the enemy's camp with a sword under his cloak. He told them that he had visited the camp of the Leinstermen, and that while he was away his hut had been destroyed and plundered. Aed promised him twenty cows if he himself should escape from the expedition, and bade him go to the royal pavilion where he would be fed and well treated.

'"What are the Leinstermen doing?" said the king. "They are preparing food for you, and you never got food more satisfying. They are boiling their swine and their beeves and their bacon."

'"A curse on him!" said Cenél Eogain and Cenél Conaill. "I see a warrior's eyes in the leper's head," said the king. "It is unhappy for you to have set your heart on the kingship of Ireland, if you fear my eyes," [said the leper]. "That is not what I fear," said the king. "Send for Dub Dúin, king of Oriel." Then Dub Dúin came up. The king of Ireland said to him: "Go", said the king of Ireland, "with the army of Oriel south to Bun Aife and to the Cruadaball, and stand guard there so that the Leinstermen may not attack our camp."'

Then Aed son of Ainmire called for the cowl of St. Colum Cille that he might wear it as a protection against the Leinstermen, for Colum Cille had promised him that he should not be slain while he wore the cowl.

[1] Giraldus Cambrensis reports the custom of parties to covenants drinking each other's blood, *Top. Hib.* III xxii.

(95–104) (Here there is a digression reporting the conversation of Aed with Colum Cille. The saint names three kings who have attained heaven: Daimín Damargait,[1] king of Oriel, who was generous to clerics and to the Church; Ailill Inbanna,[2] king of Connacht, who gave his life to save his army; Feradach the Fair,[3] king of Ossory, a miser who repented. Aed asks shall he obtain heaven and is told that he shall not. Then he requests that he may at least be victorious over the Leinstermen.[4] 'I find that difficult,' said Colum Cille, 'for my mother is one of them, and the Leinstermen came to me to Durrow and fasted against me so that I should give them the gift of a sister's son, and what they asked of me was that no foreign king should triumph over them, and I made them that promise. However, here is my cowl for you, and you shall never be killed while it is about you.')

(105) This was the cowl that Aed called for now, but it had been left behind in Ailech. Aed foresaw that he would be killed that night.

(106–19) Meanwhile Brandub's preparations were made, and he moved forward. His force encountered the men of Oriel, who challenged them, but they said that they were bringing food to the king of Ireland. The men of Oriel felt the baskets and found only the food. The king of Oriel gave orders to let them pass, and his men followed them to the camp lest they should lose their share of the feast. The Leinstermen marched into the middle of the camp. Then the cauldron was removed from the torch. 'What is the great light that we see?' said the king of Ireland. 'The food which has arrived,' said the leper. Then he arose, took off his wooden leg, and grasped his sword. The oxen were unloaded and the wild horses turned loose, so that the horses of the men of Ireland stampeded and broke up the camp. The Leinstermen arose out of their baskets and put the men of Ireland to flight, so that even Cenél Eogain and Cenél Conaill did not stand. A hedge of spears and shields was made around the king of Ireland, and he was put on his horse and

---

[1] He is the ancestor of Síl Daimini in the country of the Uí Gentig, LL 341a 33–44. His death is recorded AU 564. He was drowned as a child and restored to life by St. Maedóc, VSH ii 143–4.

[2] Tigernach, RC 17, 139 = FM 544.

[3] Tigernach, RC 17, 154 = FM 582.

[4] It was of course a standing feud, as this whole text explains.

taken to Berna na Sciath ('The Gap of the Shields'). There the
men of Ireland lost their shields. Rón Cerr attacked the king,
and killed nine of his bodyguard. Dub Dúin, king of Oriel, came
against him and was slain. Fergus, king of Tulach Óc, suffered
the same fate. Then Rón Cerr dragged the king from his horse,
and cut off his head. He poured the scraps of food from his
wallet and put the head into it, and he went away on to the
mountain-side and stayed there till morning.[1] The men of
Ireland were routed with slaughter. On the morrow Rón Cerr
came to Brandub and laid the head of Aed son of Ainmire before
him. 'So that is the Battle of the Pass of Dún Bolg for the
Bórama, and the Death of Aed son of Ainmire. Although Aed
fell on account of the *Bórama*, he levied it twice without a
battle.'[2]

(121–4) (There follows a list of kings of Ireland covering a
period of some seventy years, all of whom levied the Tribute,
apparently without opposition. The last names are those of
Bláthmac and Diarmait, who appear in the tale of Cano son
of Gartnán. Then Sechnasach son of Bláthmac became king,[3]
and he failed to levy it, being defeated in battle. He was succeeded by Cennfaelad son of Crundmael,[4] who levied it twice by
force. Cennfaelad was slain by Finnachta the Festive son of
Dunchad.)[5]

(125–30) Finnachta was king of Ireland for twenty years, and
levied the Tribute twice without opposition, but the third time
that he came to levy it the Leinstermen resisted. Bran son of
Conall was then king of Leinster, and armies were assembled on
both sides. St. Mo Ling was then at Ros Brocc[6] where he had
established himself, whence it is now called Tech Mo Ling.
Messengers were sent to him, and he came to Ailenn[7] where the
Leinstermen were mustered. He was made welcome and sat on
the right hand of the king. Tuathal son of Ailill, king of Uí

[1] The death of Aed is credited to Brandub himself in the Latin life of St.
Maedóc, VSH ii 149.
[2] Lecan (fcs. 308a21) here quotes two stanzas attributed to Aed's wife, one
of which has been edited by Meyer, *Bruchstücke* 37: 'Dear were the three sides
which I never more hope to visit, the side of Tara, the side of Teltown, and the
side of Aed son of Ainmire.'   [3] Tigernach, RC 17, 199 = FM 664.
[4] Tigernach, RC 17, 202 = FM 670.
[5] Tigernach, RC 17, 203 = FM 673.
[6] Ross Bruicc is here the form, as frequently.
[7] Knockaulin, County Kildare.

Muiredaig, proposed that Mo Ling be sent to ask for remission of the Tribute.

(Here in a poem the conversation of Bran, Tuathal, and Mo Ling is narrated. Bran calls upon Tuathal to declare who will deliver the Leinstermen, and recites a whole litany of names of Leinster saints, ending with Mo Ling. Or must the princes of Leinster fall in battle? Tuathal answers that Mo Ling, 'the blazing flame, the wave that floods the eastern coasts', will serve them well. Mo Ling son of Faillén is a banner over the hosts, a well steered ship, the kalends of the month, the star of Ros Brocc, the Daniel of the Gaedil. Mo Ling responds with a promise that he will go, and that the Tribute will not be levied. Bran bids him go and promises him rich rewards, his horse and his cloak, and a territory of land for him and his son and grandson. Mo Ling answers that this generosity will bring Bran lasting fame. He promises success and recalls the past victories of the Leinstermen.)

(131–44) Mo Ling set out, taking with him Tollchenn of Cluain Ena, a *fili*, to recite for him the poem that he had composed for Finnachta. They spent the night at the house of Cobthach son of Colmán in Uíb Faeláin, and while they were there the retinue of the *fili* said to him that they thought it shameful that he should himself be in the retinue of a cleric. Tollchenn accordingly went on alone to visit Finnachta, and when Mo Ling arose on the morrow he found that Tollchenn was gone. He went on his way and was met by a band of youths headed by Donngilla son of Finnachta, who pelted him with sods and stones. When he reached the king's house, he was not received with honour. Then a swift retribution was visited upon Donngilla, for he was killed by a stray shot aimed at a deer, and the men of Ireland raised a great cry of lamentation. Finnachta asked the reason for this cry. 'Your son Donngilla has fallen for dishonouring me,' said Mo Ling. Finnachta besought the saint to restore his son to life, and promised a reward. 'For my poem, and for restoring your son and for granting heaven to yourself,' said Mo Ling, 'I ask only the remission of the *Bórama* till *Luan*.' 'You shall have it,' said the king. Mo Ling then bound him by the Blessed Trinity and the Four Gospels, and recited his poem. Finnachta protested that the saint had lied in reciting Tollchenn's poem as his own. Mo Ling challenged

Tollchenn to recite the poem if it was he that had composed it. Tollchenn arose and tried to recite it, but nonsense came from his lips. Then a blast of wind swept him northwards to Fanaid, north of Assarroe, and he was drowned in the sea. Finnachta did reverence to Mo Ling, and begged him to restore his son and accept what he had demanded. Mo Ling stood over the boy and prayed fervently to the Lord, and God restored the son of Finnachta to life. The saint's prayer over Donngilla is in verse, and in it he says:

'The *Luan* that was named shall be Mo Ling's *Luan*. It shall be a long delay, not a delay that expires: it shall not be the *Luan* of time (Monday), but the *Luan* of eternity (Doomsday).'

(145–62) Mo Ling returned to the Leinstermen after the *Bórama* had been remitted. And Adamnán heard the report that the *Bórama* had been remitted till *Luan*, and came to visit Finnachta. He sent a cleric to the king to bid him come into his presence. The king was playing chess and refused to come until he had finished his game. The saint sent back a message that he would recite fifty psalms meanwhile, and that one of those psalms would deprive his descendants and any of his name of the kingship for ever. The king paid no heed until that game was over. He was summoned again, and again he refused to go until the next game was played. The saint sent a message that he would recite another fifty psalms, and that one of those psalms would shorten the king's life. Finnachta paid no heed until that game was finished. He was again bidden to come, and a third time he refused until he should play another game. 'Tell him,' said Adamnán, 'that I shall recite fifty psalms meanwhile, and that there is a psalm among them that will take away from him the Lord's mercy.' Then Finnachta put away the chess and came in haste. God did not will that Adamnán should deprive him of what Mo Ling had promised.

Adamnán explained to the king that he had been deceived, for the *Luan* Mo Ling intended was the Day of Judgement, and that unless he revoked the remission of the *Bórama* that day, it could never be revoked. He then recited a poem reproaching Finnachta for remitting the *Bórama*, and praising the wisdom and holiness of Mo Ling. The men of Ireland resolved to pursue

Mo Ling, and set out after him. Mo Ling saw them coming and uttered a poem calling upon the Lord to restrain Finnachta and pronouncing a curse upon him. He then struck his bell and frightened the cattle so that every beast fled into the wilderness. But the men of Ireland surrounded them. Mo Ling's extremity was revealed to Mo Thairén who was at the court of the king of Leinster, and he prayed that a mist might be cast around Mo Ling and his companions (and presumably the cattle). A mist came about them, so that they were invisible to the enemy, although they did not know it. Mo Ling went to Áth Loegaire where Labraid Loingsech was born, and saw the abbey of Kildare close by. He uttered a poem in prayer to Saint Brigid and others of the saints of Ireland to protect him against his enemies.

Finnachta, having been cursed by Mo Ling, was slain at Grellach Dollaid by Aed son of Ailill son of Aed Sláine and by Congal son of Conang son of Congal son of Aed Sláine.

THE ALLEGORY OF URARD MAC COISE

Finally there is a text which deserves mention, although it hardly belongs to the historical cycles. Its chief importance, for the story is tedious, lies in the fact that it contains one of the two surviving recensions of an old list of sagas.[1] The allegorical form is of interest, since this is the earliest example in Irish secular literature.

The text is preserved in RIA 23 N 10 (16th century), Rawl. B 512 (f. 109, 14th century) and Harl. 5280 (f. 58, 16th century). It has not yet been translated. The language is very obscure, although it can hardly be earlier than the eleventh century. Only a scholar experienced in the language of the legal tracts would be able to make an adequate translation.

Ed. Mary E. Byrne (N with variants from R and H), *Anecdota* ii 42–76.

(1–9) The gist of the story is that the home of the poet Urard Mac Coise († 990) was plundered by Cenél Eogain, and the poet went to complain to the king of Ireland, Domnall son of Muirchertach († 980). The king asked him to tell a story, and the poet bade him choose from among the chief stories of Ireland. The king asked him to name them, so that he might make his choice, and so the list is introduced. First there is a group of common stories (*gnáthscéla*), then Cattle-Raids (*tánai*), then Adventures (*echtrai*), Birth-Tales (*coimperta*), Battles (*catha*), Plunderings (*togla*), Feasts (*fesa*), Frenzies (*buili*), Wooings (*tochmarca*), Elopements (*aithid*), (a second group of *togla*), Floods (*tomadmann*), Visions (*físi*), Love-Tales (*serca*), Hostings (*slúagid*), Invasions (*tochomlada*), and Destructions (*orcni*). At the end of the last group the poet adds an imaginary title: *Orgain Cathrach Mail Milscothaig maic Anma Airmiten maic Sochoisc Sochuide maic Ollaman Airchetail maic Dána Dligedaig maic Lugdach Ildánaig maic Rúaid Rofesa maic Creidme In Spirda Naím Athar sceo Maic*, 'The Destruction of the Citadel of Mael Milscothach son of Reverend Soul son of Discipline of Society son of Professor of Poetry son of Regular

---

[1] Thurneysen discusses the relationship between the two recensions, and recognizes a common source, which he assigns to the tenth century, *Heldensage* 21.

Verse son of Lugaid of Many Arts son of Strength of Wisdom son of Faith in The Holy Ghost, The Father and The Son.'

'For the name that Mac Coise gave himself to conceal his identity was Mael Milscothach, that is "of sweet words", for *scoth* means "word" and "speech" in Irish.'

The king asked Mac Coise to tell this tale for he had never heard it. And so the story proper begins.

(10–25) The story is told as a sort of allegory, with lists of fanciful names for the persons involved, and in obscure poetic diction. When the outrage has been told, and the injured poet is said to have resorted to the king of Ireland of the time, who promises him full redress, it is revealed that that king is none other than Domnall son of Muirchertach son of Niall son of Aed, and that Mael Milscothach is Urard son of Coise of Connacht.

(26–33) When the king hears this he sends Warning son of Proclamation with horsemen to apprehend the robbers. They are overtaken while dividing the spoil, and Warning addresses them in a long poem. Merriment son of Justice replies in a poem, promising that the plunder shall be restored, and Mael Milscothach in a third poem boasts of his friendship for Domnall.[1] The king summons the princes of Cenél Eogain to take counsel about the outrage, and they speak nobly and generously. The king may punish the guilty as he will, but for their part they will give the poet a cow from each lord and royal retainer. The king then pronounces a decision favourable to Mael Milscothach in very obscure legal language. He apparently invites the *brethemuin* and *senchaidi*, *filid* whose special studies were law and history respectively, to decide what fine and honour-price should be paid. The *senchaidi*,[2] both *filid* and *brethemuin*, ask Fland, *fer legind* of Clonmacnoise to appoint the fine and honour-price. He pronounces judgement in alliterative legal language, the sense of which is not clear to me. Mael Milscothach receives compensation according to the decision of the learned men, in addition to the restoration of his property. And they decide that every *ollam* who can practise the three arts of judgement known as *imbas forosndai*,[3] *dichetal do chollaib cenn*

---

[1] The allegorical names seem out of place here, as the allegory is at an end.

[2] Here *senchaid* is used as a generic term to include poets and lawyers.

[3] On this means of divination s. Thurneysen, ZCP 19, 163.

and *teinm laída*[1] shall be entitled to the same honour-price as the king of Tara in atonement for wrongs suffered by him.

This is chronologically the latest of the historical sagas. We have seen indeed that Brian Bórama (†1014) is mentioned in 'The Adventure of the Sons of Eochu Muigmedón' (*sup.*, p. 40), but there is no cycle connected specially with his name. The long historical tract entitled *Cogadh Gaedhel re Gallaibh* does not belong to the saga-literature. It is an account of the rise of the Dalcassians of Munster under Brian Bórama, and of the great battle of Clontarf (A.D. 1014) in which the Irish defeated the Norse. Even here the convention of introducing long poems into the text is observed in the later manuscript.[2] But the text is not a saga but a history. Its author may have been prompted by the translations of Latin historical works which were made about the twelfth century. One story about Brian's time may be mentioned here, namely *Léiges Coise Chéin* ('The Healing of Cian's Leg'). It is preserved in a manuscript of the late fifteenth century (BM Eg. 1781 f. 147), but in form it is a modern romantic frame-story of the type common in contemporary Irish folk-lore.[3]

The amount of history that is enshrined in these stories is still a matter for investigation. We have seen that some of them are plainly fiction, since they bring together historical persons who were not contemporaries. Others have been held to be mere legend or mythology. Professor O'Rahilly has recently declared that Lugaid Mac Con is a divine ancestor of the Érainn, a Munster dynasty.[4] But even the legendary tales contain information about the political framework of Ireland as it was witnessed or remembered by the writers, and a certain amount of history. The statement that a king of Dál Araide and a king of Dál Fiatach were joint kings of Ulster (*Ulaid*) in the

---

[1] The three arts are discussed by R. D. Scott, *The Thumb of Knowledge*, chap. iii; s. also Thurneysen, *Heldensage* 71.

[2] The fragment in LL (fcs. 309–10) does not include the relevant passages.

[3] RIA Stowe B iv 1 (f. 180, 17th century) also preserves it, s. O'Rahilly, *Gadelica*, i 279; Flower, *Catalogue* 541. It has been edited and translated by O'Grady, SG i 296 = ii 332. Goedheer supplies a list of folk-tales in which Brian is the hero, *Irish and Norse Traditions about the Battle of Clontarf* 71, note 1.

[4] 'The Goidels and their predecessors', *Proc. Brit. Acad.* xxi 336; cf. *Ériu* 13, 152; 153, note 1.

seventh century (p. 51) is of some interest. The close contact that existed with the Irish kingdom in Scotland, sometimes regarded as a province of Ireland, and even with the Britons of Strathclyde, is in the background of many of the tales that we have considered. The manners and customs described are not dependent upon the historical accuracy of the story in which they appear.

My growing impression, as I have studied these stories, and referred from time to time to annals and genealogies and historical tracts, to verify a tradition or to fix a date, has been that there is a great deal of history in them. For the present almost everything about the political history of Ireland prior to the tenth century is doubtful. It seems to me likely, however, that the historians of the future will discover that Conn of the Hundred Battles and Eogan Mór and Cathaer Már, king of Leinster, and the famous Cormac Mac Airt were historical persons, and that a fairly reliable historical tradition can be established from as early a time as the second century of the Christian era.

INDEXES

PERSONS

TITLES

Aided Crimthainn maic Fidaig (The Death of Crimthann son of Fidach), 30–3.
Aided Maele Fothartaig (The Death of Mael Fothartaig), 35, 42–8.
Aided Meic Con (The Death of Mac Con), 16, 22.
Airecc Menman Uraird Maic Coise (The Allegory of Urard Mac Coise), 115–17.
Aisling Meic Con Glinne (The Vision of Mac Con Glinne), 99.
Amra Choluim(b) Chille (The Eulogy of Colum Cille), 7, 61, 91.
Auraicept na nÉces (The Scholars' Primer), 56.

Baile Binnbérlach Mac Buain (Baile of the Clear Voice son of Buan), 27–9.
Baile Chuind Chétchathaig (The Frenzy of Conn of the Hundred Battles), 12.
Baile in Scáil (The Phantom's Frenzy), 11–14, 22.
Betha Ruadáin (The Life of Ruadán), 58.
Bórama (The Tribute), 4, 99, 100, 103–14.
Branwen ferch Llyr (Branwen daughter of Llyr), 4.
Buile Shuibne (The Frenzy of Suibne), 56, 65, 68–74.

Cáin Domnaig (The Law of Sunday), 76.
Caithréim Cellaig (The Noble Career of Cellach), 81, 83–9.
Cath Almaine (The Battle of Allen), 99–102.
Cath Belaig Dúin Bolg (The Battle of Belach Dúin Bolg), 55, 103.
Cath Cairn Chonaill (The Battle of Carn Conaill), 75, 78, 81.
Cath Cind Abrat (The Battle of Cend Abrat), 18.
Cath Crinna (The Battle of Crinna), 22, 25.
Cath Maige Léna (The Battle of Mag Léna), 11.
Cath Maige Mucrama (The Battle of Mag Mucrama), 15, 16–22, 23, 35, 39, 57.
Cath Maige Rátha (The Battle of Moira), 56, 65–8.
Cogadh Gaedhel re Gallaibh (The War of the Gaedheal against the Gall), 117.
Cóir Anmann (The Fitness of Names), 7, 16, 20, 38.
Compert Mongáin 7 Serc Duibe Lacha do Mongán (The Birth of Mongán and His Love for Dub Lacha), 49–55.
Cormac's Glossary, 30.

Dindshenchas (The History of Places), 19, 21, 22, 25, 38, 83, 88.

Echtra Cormaic i Tír Tairngiri (The Adventure of Cormac in the Land of Promise), 28.
Echtra Mac nEchach Mugmedóin (The Adventure of the Sons of Eochu Mugmedón), 38–41, 117.
Erchoitmed Ingine Gulidi (The Excuse of Gulide's Daughter), 33–4.
Esnada Tige Buchet (The Melodies of Buchet's House), 25–7.

Fástini Airt meic Cuind (The Prophecy of Art son of Conn), 22.
Fingal Rónáin, see *Aided Maele Fothartaig*.
Fled Dúin na nGéd (The Feast of Dún na nGéd), 20, 31, 41, 56, 57–64, 92.

Gein Branduib meic Echach 7 Aeddin meic Gabráin (The Birth-Tales of Brandub son of Eochu and Aedán son of Gabrán), 41, 49, 64.
Geineamain Chormaic (The Birth of Cormac), 23–5, 39.

Imram Curaig Maele Dúin (The Voyage of Mael Dúin's Coracle), 24.

Kulhwch ac Olwen (Kulhwch and Olwen), 7.

Lebor Gabála Érenn (The Book of Invasions), 1.
Léiges Coise Chéin (The Healing of Cian's Leg), 117.
Longes Chonaill Chuirc (The Exile of Conall Corc), 34–7, 88.

MANUSCRIPTS